English for Academic Study:

Extended Writing & Research Skills

Course Book

Joan McCormack and John Slaght

University of **Reading**

CALS
Centre for
Applied Language Studies

Garnet
EDUCATION

Credits

Published by
Garnet Publishing Ltd.
8 Southern Court
South Street
Reading RG1 4QS, UK

This edition first published 2005.
Reprinted 2007, 2008.
Fully revised 2009.

ISBN 978 1 85964 486 7

British Cataloguing-in-Publication Data
A catalogue record for this book is available from the British Library.

Production
Project manager: Simone Davies
Project consultant: Rod Webb
Editorial team: Penny Analytis, Jo Caulkett, Chris Gough, Fiona McGarry, Nicky Platt
Art director: Mike Hinks
Design: Nick Asher
Photography: Corbis: Adrian Arbib, Pallova Bagla, Yann Arthus-Bertrand, Bloomimage, Adrian Bradshaw/epa, Goldberg Diego, Fancy/Veer, Peter Guttman, George Hall, Lee Jae-Won, Martin Jones-Ecoscene, Frans Lanting, Robert Landau, David Lawrence, Lester Lefkowitz, Stephanie Maze, Tim Pannell, Kevin R. Morris, Reuters, Royalty-Free, Norbert Schaefer; Getty Images: BlueJean Images, Jon Feingersh, Gorilla Creative Images, Jupiter Images, David de Lossy, Picturegarden, Júlía Runólfsdóttir, Sami Sarkis, Southern Stock, Paul Thomas, Ofer Wolberger, James Woodson.

Printed and bound
in Great Britain by Cambrian Printers Ltd, Aberystwyth, Wales.

The authors and publishers wish to acknowledge the following use of material:

W. M. Adams, Andrew Jordan & Tim O'Riordan, ed. P. Cloke et. al., *Introducing human geographies*, Arnold, 1999. Reproduced by permission of Hodder Arnold.

Contemporary international relations, Papp, D., © Pearson Education. Reprinted by permission of Pearson Education, Inc.

Extract from 'Safety in numbers' by A. Barnett and 'Can LA kick the car habit?' by Dan Thisdell reproduced with permission from *New Scientist*.

'Banking system developments in the four Asian tigers' by Chan Huh, reprinted from the Federal Reserve Bank of San Francisco *Economic Letter* 97–122. The opinions expressed in this article do not necessarily reflect the views of the management of the Federal Bank of San Francisco, or of the Board of Governors of the Federal Reserve System.

Leisure and tourism, Youell, R. © Pearson Education Limited. Reprinted by permission of Pearson Education, Inc.

Crown copyright material is reproduced with the permission of the Controller of HMSO and the Queen's Printer for Scotland.

Core geography, Naish et al. © Pearson Education Limited. Reprinted by permission of Pearson Education, Inc.

An introduction to sustainable development, 1999, Routledge.

'Reducing automobile dependence' © Peter Newman. Reproduced by permission of the author.

Contents

Book map

Topic	Tasks

1   Introduction to the skills of extended writing and research

- Critical thinking in academic study
- What do students in higher education write?
- Types of writing
- Participating in a tutorial: getting help with writing
- Analyzing the task
- The stages of writing a project
- Starting Project 1: ideas for the introduction, main body and conclusion
- Unit Summary

2   Using evidence to support your ideas

- Selective reading: reading for research purposes
- Incorporating evidence into academic work
- Referencing: direct quotations, summaries and paraphrases
- Purposeful reading: searching texts for definitions
- Features of a summary
- Stages in writing a summary or paraphrase
- Practice summary 1
- Practice summary 2
- Practice summary 3
- Unit Summary

3   Structuring your project and finding information

- The structure of projects
- Descriptive and evaluative writing
- Reading for a specific purpose
- Choosing sources
- Finding information
- Analyzing websites: critical evaluation
- Acknowledging your sources
- Academic conventions in referencing
- When to avoid using online sources
- Writing a bibliography
- Unit Summary

4   Developing your project

- Preparing for tutorials: discussing feedback on draft text
- Quotations, paraphrases and plagiarism
- Avoiding plagiarism
- Working with abstracts
- Unit Summary

5   Developing a focus

- Choosing a topic for your extended essay
- Developing a topic
- Establishing a focus
- Establishing a working title
- Planning Project 2
- Unit Summary

Topic	Tasks
6 • Introductions, conclusions and definitions	• Features of introductions
	• Analyzing your introduction
	• The language of introductions
	• Identifying the thesis statement
	• Features of conclusions
	• Analyzing your conclusion
	• The language of conclusions
	• Features of definitions
	• Unit Summary
7 • Incorporating data and illustrations	• The purpose of data
	• The language used for incorporating data
	• Data commentary
	• The language of data commentary
	• Practice data commentary
	• Unit Summary
8 • Preparing for conference presentations and editing your work	• Features of abstracts
	• Conference abstracts
	• Preparing an oral presentation
	• Preparing a poster presentation
	• Unit Summary

Acknowledgements

The creation of these materials stemmed from the need to help international students develop the study skills necessary to function effectively on academic courses in a university context. The rationale behind the material is that students need to develop the confidence and competence to become autonomous learners in order to successfully carry out research and complete assignments, such as extended pieces of written work or oral presentations.

The development of these materials has been a collaborative effort which goes far beyond the collaboration between the authors. The material has evolved over several years of pre-sessional teaching at the Centre for Applied Language Studies at the University of Reading. There have been significant additions from a number of teachers, who have either contributed ideas or given extensive feedback on the materials. The number of teachers involved is too large for us to mention each one individually, but they are all fully appreciated.

In something like their present form, the materials have been trialled on successive pre-sessional courses at the University of Reading since 2001. This trialling has involved almost a thousand students, and they too have provided feedback in terms of course evaluation, as well as with their responses to the tasks in the programme. We very much appreciate the contribution of students whose work has been adapted and incorporated into the materials.

We would particularly like to thank Jill Riley for her meticulous editing and typing up of the materials and Corinne Boz and Bruce Howell for their contributions.

Particular mention should also be made of our colleague Sarah Brewer, for her ideas selflessly shared, her knowledge of referencing and academic conventions and her patient and meticulous editing – not to mention the seven years she has spent teaching and commenting upon the contents of this book.

Finally, we would like to acknowledge the contribution of Mansoor Alhagbani, who gave us permission to publish his extended essay, *To what extent should insider dealing be regulated, and how can this be done effectively?*, on pages 109–118.

Joan McCormack and John Slaght, authors, April 2009

Referencing

The system of referencing in the book is that of the APA (American Psychological Association). See a brief summary in Appendix 5.

A number of the sources included have used different systems; these have been reproduced in the original form. It is worth pointing this out to students, and ensuring they follow the APA system consistently in their own writing of projects.

However, individual institutions or groups may well have their own system. It is important to be systematic and meticulous in the choice and use of the system decided on. Obviously it is not possible to move between different systems.

Introduction

EAS Extended Writing & Research Skills has been designed with the aims of helping you to:
● improve your extended writing and research skills;
● develop an independent approach to extended writing and research.

The purposes of this textbook are to support you in developing your extended writing and research skills and to encourage the development of an independent approach to extended writing and research. It is assumed that you will be working on the development and consolidation of core academic written language skills on other parts of your course, and part of the aim of these materials is to put such skills into practice.

The book is designed around a ten-week course, during which you are expected to write two projects: a guided project in the first four weeks, and a project in your own academic subject over the remaining six weeks. You will be working on the projects at the same time as you carry out the tasks in each unit of this book.

There is a suggested route through the materials for a shorter course of, for example, six weeks. In this case, you are encouraged to study the materials that are not covered on your course, independently.

The course is designed so that for Project 1, the whole group will be working on the same essay title, which is provided in the book along with appropriate source material. Your teacher will support you in planning and writing this project, which will enable you to develop the skills you need for extended academic writing.

Alternatively, especially on a short course, your teacher might choose to go straight to Project 2 (see below).

In academic life at university, students are expected to work independently, and in Project 2 this aspect is emphasized. With the second project, you have to choose your own title and decide on the focus of the project. Although you will need to find your own resources, you will, of course, be supported in class and in tutorials during this period. For example, you will be able to 'negotiate' a title in collaboration with your tutor and make changes to your project after discussing your work with her/him at various stages of the project.

The differences between Project 1 and Project 2

	Project 1	Project 2
Title	Given in textbook	Your choice of topic in your subject area
Length	About 1,200 words	2,000–3,000 words
Resources	Mostly provided in the book	You need to find your own
Support	A lot of support provided in the book and by your teacher	Working more independently, with tutorials

This course will help you to develop a number of skills while writing your projects. These include the following:

- brainstorming and planning your work;

- establishing a specific focus and developing your ideas;

- finding sources of information from books, journals and the Internet;

- selecting information appropriate to your needs;

- incorporating ideas and information into your text through paraphrasing/summarizing and synthesizing, while avoiding plagiarism;

- evaluating your sources and selecting the most relevant and appropriate;

- developing your critical thinking skills;

- learning about UK academic conventions for referencing and compiling a bibliography;

- discussing your work with your tutor and your peers;

- giving a presentation about your work.

One aspect of extended writing that students often find particularly difficult is expressing their ideas in their own words; that is to say, establishing their own voice. This course will explore ways to help you achieve this, in particular by encouraging a system that ensures you avoid lifting sections directly from the original sources and copying them into your own extended writing projects. Understanding how to avoid plagiarism and develop your own voice is essential in academic writing. Apart from the fact that plagiarism is considered serious misconduct, expressing your own ideas illustrates that you have evaluated your sources and understood their full meaning. It also demonstrates that the ideas and information that you do quote directly have been chosen for a particularly significant reason.

Additional interactive activities to accompany these materials can be found online, at www.englishforacademicstudy.com.

Introduction to the skills of extended writing and research

In this unit you will:
- be introduced to extended writing and what it involves;
- find out about writing a project.

Introduction

Academic disciplines on the typical university campus

There are a number of schools (or faculties) on university campuses, and within these, there are departments and units. This page from the University of Coventry's website gives an example of how universities are usually structured.

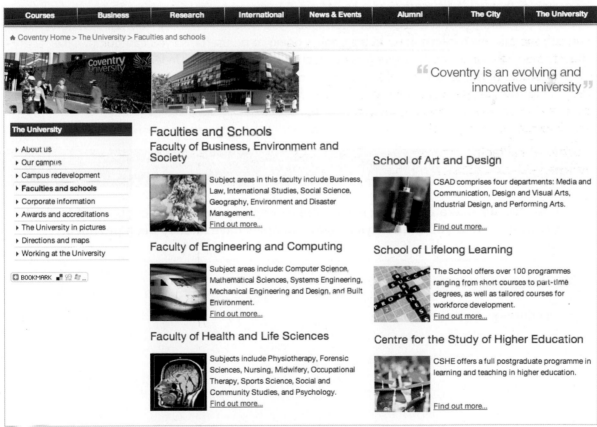

Source: Coventry University. (2009). Retrieved April 27, 2009, from Coventry University website: http://www.coventry.ac.uk/University/Pages/Facultiesandschools.aspx

Students usually have to produce a specific type of written assignment, on which they are assessed, and this normally differs according to the requirements of their academic department. The type of writing that students have to produce also depends on the level of study: whether *undergraduate, postgraduate* or *doctoral (PhD)*.

Extended writing at university: why do students write?

Students write for a number of purposes, according to the particular requirements of their course. In many cases, the topic or title will be predetermined by the lecturer and may require the reading of recommended texts. At other times – for example, when writing a thesis or dissertation – students have to choose their own titles. Students will receive guidelines and support from a supervisor, but on the whole, they are expected to work independently at this level.

The reasons why students carry out extended academic writing activities may include the following:

• to develop and express their ideas;

• to provide evidence to support their ideas;

• to show they can dispute or support existing theories (which involves demonstrating their *critical thinking* ability);

• to display knowledge.

The type of writing required is determined by the *purpose* of the writing.

Key research and writing skills: Critical thinking is an important feature of academic study. Imagine, for example, that you have borrowed a book from the university library that has to be returned the following day, but it contains important information you need for an essay. You will have to think 'critically' about which information in the book is going to be useful, so you can quickly take appropriate notes or photocopies, i.e., use your critical thinking skills. Understanding what is relevant is one example of the ability to think critically. Another example of critical thinking is recognizing the writer's *purpose*, or reason for writing a text, e.g., whether it is to inform, to persuade, or to support or refute a viewpoint.

Task 1: Critical thinking

In the box below, make a list of at least three examples of what you might need to think about critically when you are studying. Two examples have already been provided.

> **a)** Recognizing relevant information
>
> **b)** Identifying the writer's purpose
>
> **c)** _____
>
> **d)** _____
>
> **e)** _____

Task 2: What do students in higher education write?

You are going to brainstorm some ideas about the kind of writing students have to do at university. This involves writing down as many ideas as you can about the topic. You are going to do this very quickly, within a time limit, so don't be concerned about the accuracy of your grammar or spelling.

2.1 **Work with a partner. Brainstorm the kinds of writing students have to do at university.**

Note your ideas in the box below, without worrying about how you write, the order of ideas, etc. One idea has been written for you as an example.

WHAT STUDENTS HAVE TO WRITE AT UNIVERSITY

- *Reports of experiments*
-
-
-
-
-

2.2 **Now read the explanation below of the types of writing expected of students in higher education. Compare them with your own ideas.**

University students are often asked to write *essays*. These may be as short as 600 words, especially during examinations. However, undergraduate students as well as postgraduate students are also frequently required to write *extended essays*. A typical length for an extended essay is 2,500–3,000 words. We sometimes refer to these extended essays as *projects*.

Towards the end of their period of study, most students will be expected to write either a *thesis* or a *dissertation*. Collins Cobuild Advanced Learner's English Dictionary defines a dissertation as "a long piece of writing based on the writer's own ideas and research as part of a university degree, especially a higher degree such as a PhD". In the United Kingdom and Ireland, a dissertation is often written for a master's-level degree.

According to the University of London website, a thesis is the:

acquisition and dissemination of new knowledge. In order to demonstrate this the author must demonstrate an understanding of what the relevant state of the art is and what are the strengths and weaknesses of this situation. For someone's work to be knowledge there must be a demonstration that suitable and systematic methods were used to evaluate the chosen hypothesis.

http://www.cs.ucl.ac.uk/staff/c.clack/phd.html

Not all students are required to write traditional-style essays. For example, in the Engineering Department of a university, students will often be expected to write *reports* on projects they have been working on during their course.

In certain academic disciplines, such as Applied Linguistics, Education or Sociology, students may be required to write a *case study*. A good example of a case study might be the "study of speech, writing, or language use of one person, either at one point in time or over a period of time, e.g., a child over a period of one year" (Richards, Platt & Weber, 1985, p. 36). A student in an Applied Linguistics Department would probably write a case study like this.

Students also have to write *notes*: from written sources, or when attending a lecture, seminar or tutorial. Some students *annotate* lecture handouts, either by highlighting key points or by writing notes/comments in the margins of the text, which may be useful later.

2.3 Discuss with a partner what types of writing you expect to do on your university courses in the future.

Task 3: Types of writing

Complete the table below to clarify your understanding of the types of writing described on page 11.

Type of writing	Type of student	Explanation
essay for an examination		traditional 600–1,000-word text written during an exam
non-examination essay		written work submitted as part of the course requirement during term time – typically 600–6,000 words
report		
dissertation		
thesis		
case study		
notes		
annotations		

Writing as a common process

Whatever form of extended writing students are expected to do, the process will usually involve the following steps:

- gathering information from various sources;
- organizing this information so that it appropriately answers the needs of the task that the writer has to complete;
- planning the text;
- drafting and redrafting the text until it communicates the information and ideas fully and clearly.

Types of assessment

The writing of reports, case studies, dissertations and theses forms part of the assessment process in most academic disciplines in universities. Another means of assessment is *oral presentations*. Presentations are normally given as part of a study project. For example, a student writing a report might give a presentation in order to 'present' her/his report in a clear, concise way. Oral presentations can be given by an individual student, or they can be group presentations.

Another form of presentation is the *poster presentation*. In this case, the student prepares a visual display outlining the work or project s/he has been involved in. A poster presentation will normally be given during a student conference. Students display their work, and participants and visitors to the conference are invited to look at the display and ask the author of the poster questions about the process or information they can see. At the same time, other students will be giving oral presentations at the conference. You will do further work on presentations later in this book (see Unit 8).

Apart from the methods of written and oral assessment mentioned above, of course, students will probably have to take exams at the end of term and/or the end of year, as well as at the end of their university studies, when they take their final examinations.

Writing projects

You will do most of the extended writing for this course independently, outside the classroom. Any writing that goes on in the classroom will normally be for editing purposes, when you will have an opportunity to consult your tutor and redraft your work accordingly. You will be expected to follow a process writing approach (see *English for academic studies: Writing*, Course Book pages 7–8, for a full explanation of this term). This approach includes editing your work, submitting your first draft and redrafting the project after your tutor has given you feedback.

> This course book is designed to be used for applying the skills and strategies that you have already studied and developed in more general writing and reading classes, i.e., skills such as skimming and scanning, structuring an essay and writing a conclusion.

You might also have the opportunity to take part in one-to-one tutorials with your tutor, in order to discuss the first and subsequent drafts of any extended writing that you are working on.

Task 4: Participating in a tutorial

Write down three aspects of your project that you might expect to discuss with your tutor.

a) _____

b) _____

c) _____

You will be expected to go on redrafting and revising the content of your text in order to improve it, as long as you are able to submit your final draft before any submission deadline. The process you go through while writing the project is just as important as the final product and the final grade. Writing your project gives you the opportunity to practise the academic skills and conventions you have been learning and developing on all components of your pre-sessional course.

Guided Projects 1 and 2

This course is based around a guided project on the topic of sustainable development. For this project, you will be given certain 'core' texts to consult. However, you will have the opportunity to carry out some independent research, because you can select two extra texts of your own choice from books, journals or online sources. You will need to provide hard copies of these sources for your tutor, and, of course, they must be sources written in English.

The aim of this guided project is to give you practice in finding appropriate information. Although a range of texts are available, you will need to read *selectively* in order to find information that is relevant to the task title. You will also practise taking notes from these sources, and using them as the basis for summarizing ideas and synthesizing information into your project. In addition, you will be given advice on how to avoid plagiarism and how to acknowledge the origin of your information.

Study tip

While working on projects, you should make good use of any tutorial sessions.
- Prepare questions before the tutorial.
- When working on a project in your subject area, be sure that you have a thorough knowledge of the topic you are writing about.

The guided project should be considered as practice for a second project related to your own subject area. For this second project, you should make all the decisions about the subject, topic and title, and you will carry out the research independently (including the search for appropriate sources).

Note: Your teacher might decide not to do Project 1 and simply make use of the practice activities to develop the necessary skills for completing Project 2, on a topic related to your own field of study.

Task 5: Analyzing the task

Before you begin any task, it is important to analyze carefully what it requires you to do. You will then have a very clear idea of your purpose for writing. Consider the following project title:

To what extent can the problems of urbanization be met by a policy of sustainable development?

Analyze the project title and highlight the key words and phrases. Then discuss the following with a partner.

a) How is the title framed, e.g., statement/question/heading?

b) What does the title ask you to do?

Task 6: The stages of writing a project

There are three stages in producing an extended essay or project: planning, researching and writing up. In each of these stages, there are a number of smaller steps.

6.1 Read steps a–p, below. Then write them under the appropriate stage headings on page 16, *Planning, Researching* or *Writing up*, in the most appropriate order.

Write the steps in full, not just the letters. Note that one step can be placed in two stages.

a) Read the first draft.

b) Edit the draft – decide objectively whether your ideas have been expressed clearly.

c) Think of a working title for the project. ✓

d) Search for relevant journals/books/information in the library and on the Internet.

e) Write down the details of your sources.

f) Decide if you need to do more reading.

g) Write the contents page, bibliography, title page and abstract. ✓

h) Arrange a tutorial with your tutor.

i) Do some reading.

j) Decide on a topic.

k) Write the first complete draft.

l) Highlight/take notes of relevant information. ✓

m) Plan the contents in detail.

n) Work on establishing a clear focus.

o) Make a rough outline plan of your ideas.

p) Check that sources are available/accessible.

Planning

1 _____

2 _____

3 Think of a working title for the project. _____

4 _____

5 _____

6 _____

Researching

1 _____

2 _____

3 Highlight/take notes of relevant information. _____

4 _____

5 _____

Writing up

1 _____

2 _____

3 _____

4 _____

5 Write the contents page, bibliography, title page and abstract.

6.2 Now discuss your answer with a partner. There is more than one possible order.

Task 7: Starting Project 1

In Task 5, you analyzed the title of the project *To what extent can the problems of urbanization be met by a policy of sustainable development?* You are now going to work on this project by answering a number of questions, which are grouped under three broad headings: *Introduction*, *Main body* and *Conclusion*.

> **Study tip**
>
> It is always useful to take time to ask yourself questions about an essay title, as a way of both analyzing it and brainstorming ideas. This also helps you to organize the structure of your writing.

7.1 **Read questions a–k, below, carefully and think of any possible answers.**

Introduction

a) What is 'sustainable development'? (Definition)

b) What is 'urbanization'? (Definition)

c) What are the problems of urbanization? (Background information)

d) What policies of sustainable development exist or could be introduced? (Background information)

e) To what extent do you *think* sustainable development can solve the problems?

Note: The expression *to what extent* allows you to give your opinion about the likely success of sustainable development policies. Your position (opinion) on this question will help form your *thesis* – that is the main argument you will present in your project.

Main body

f) What specific problems are related to a lack of urban space? What evidence can you find for this?

g) What specific problems are related to urban transport? What evidence can you find for this?

h) What are the possible solutions to the problems outlined above?

i) What evidence can you find to suggest that a policy of sustainable development can be successful?

Conclusion

j) Based on the evidence you have presented above, to what extent can a policy of sustainable development meet the current urban problems related to a lack of space and transport?

k) Does the evidence you put together in the 'main body' support the thesis you introduced in your introduction?

7.2 **Brainstorm some ideas on the above questions in groups.**

Write your ideas in the appropriate boxes on page 18. You need only write in note form.

At the moment, you are only being asked to guess what the answers might be. After this, you will do some reading to find out whether your guesses were appropriate. You will also be reading to find other ideas about the topic. This reading stage is one of the most important parts of your work, because you will be looking for evidence to support your ideas.

Introduction

1. _____

2. _____

3. _____

4. _____

5. _____

6. _____

Main body

1. _Lack of playground facilities for children._

2. _____

3. _____

4. _____

5. _____

6. _____

Conclusion

1. _____

2. _____

3. _____

4. _____

5. _____

6. _____

Unit Summary

In this unit, you have been introduced to the basic concept of extended writing and the types of extended writing that you may be required to produce. You have discovered what a project involves and looked at the various stages of good project writing.

1   **Using the verbs in the box below, complete these possible reasons for writing an extended project.**

dispute	develop	display	provide

a) to show that you can express and _____ ideas

b) to show that you can _____ evidence to support ideas

c) to show that you can _____ or support existing theories (which demonstrates critical thinking ability)

d) to _____ knowledge

2   **Look at the following examples of critical thinking. Mark each with either G, for *this is something I am quite good at*, or NG, for *this is something I am not so good at and I need to practise*.**

a) recognizing what is relevant and what is not relevant   ____

b) identifying the writer's purpose   ____

c) assessing the writer's argument   ____

d) comparing and evaluating issues   ____

e) evaluating the credibility of the writer's sources   ____

3   **Tick (✓) the types of extended writing that you need to practise and improve to be successful on your course.**

a) essay for an exam   ☐   **d)** thesis   ☐

b) non-examination essay   ☐   **e)** report   ☐

c) dissertation   ☐   **f)** case study   ☐

4 Look at the three stages involved in producing an extended written text, below. For each stage, write two of the steps you would need to carry out.

The first one has been done for you as an example.

a) planning   _make a rough outline plan of your ideas_

_____

b) researching   _____

_____

c) writing up   _____

_____

5 Think about the project you started in Unit 1 and answer the questions below.

a) What did you enjoy?

b) What did you find quite easy?

c) What did you find quite difficult?

For web resources relevant to this unit, see:

www.englishforacademicstudy.com/student/ewrs/links

These weblinks will provide you with ideas on how to approach different stages of the writing process, as well as links to sources on sustainable development.

2 Using evidence to support your ideas

In this unit you will:
- discuss the importance of providing evidence in academic writing;
- learn different methods of incorporating sources;
- practise summarizing information.

Introduction

Using supporting evidence

It is part of Western academic convention that any claim made in writing, e.g., an opinion or generalization, is supported by evidence. You need to show some *proof* that what you are saying is correct. You need to support any statements or points you make with *evidence*. This gives your work more *academic weight*. This is a very important aspect of Western academic convention.

Using the ideas of other people in your text and acknowledging them is an essential part of academic writing. This means referring to them twice, within the text itself and in a bibliography at the end.

In academic writing, and especially in the early stages, students are *not* expected to write their own original ideas. In fact, university departments often require students to produce written work in order to demonstrate that:

- they have read, understood and evaluated some of the literature in their field;

- they can synthesize ideas from more than one source;

- they can select appropriate academic sources to support their point of view, or perspective.

Reading list

To carry out your first project successfully, you should make use of the reading list below. The printed sources are available in Appendix 4 on page 123.

Reading list

- Adams, W.M. (1999). Sustainability. In P. Cloke, P. Crang & M. Goodwin (Eds.), *Introducing human geographies* (pp. 125–130). London: Arnold.

- Bilham-Boult, A., Blades, H., Hancock, J., Keeling, W. & Ridout, M. (1999). *People, places and themes* (pp. 202–205; p. 208). Oxford: Heinemann.

- Chaffey, J. (1994). The challenge of urbanisation. In M. Naish & S. Warn (Eds.), *Core geography* (pp. 138–146). London: Longman.

- Elliot, J.A. (1999). *An introduction to sustainable development*. London: Routledge.

- Newman, P. (1999). Transport: reducing automobile dependence. In D. Satterthwaite (Ed.), *The Earthscan reader in sustainable cities* (pp. 67–92). London: Earthscan Publications.

- Thisdell, D. (1993). Can LA kick the car habit? *New Scientist, 138*(1877), 24–29.

Task 1: Selective reading

In Task 5 of Unit 1 (page 15), you analyzed the title of the project. The next stage is to look at sources relevant to your title.

1.1 **With a partner, discuss the following questions.**

a) Why are you going to read the sources on the reading list; in other words, what is your *purpose* for reading them?

b) How are you going to read them and what reading strategies might you use?

c) What are you going to do as you read?

These questions help you to think critically as you approach your reading, i.e., you are not passively accepting any texts that you are presented with, but asking yourself questions as you read.

1.2 **Study the table below, showing reasons why you might want to read a text. Indicate how important you think each reason is by placing a tick (✓) in the appropriate column 1–5, where 1 = very important reason.**

Reasons for reading a text	1	2	3	4	5
It's on the reading list supplied by your teacher					
To compare with other texts					
Advice from tutor/lecturer/teacher					
Relevant to my purpose					
Well-known author					
To make notes					
To develop a line of enquiry					
To refute an argument					
To write everything down that's in the text					
Written by an expert in the field					
Very recently published text					
Cited in other sources					
To expand knowledge					

One of the most important things to remember about writing an academic assignment is that you are expected to frame your ideas *in your own terms*; your reader is interested in your point of view. This is true whether you are preparing to write a long dissertation or a simple summary for an oral presentation. However, you must support your point of view with evidence from the *literature* – in the case of Project 1, the sources you have read from the reading list on page 21 – or from your *fieldwork*, e.g., collecting data, or from experiments. By supporting your opinion with ideas and information from the literature, you are strengthening your viewpoint and therefore providing a more compelling argument. Such evidence is expected in academic writing.

Your purpose in reading the sources from the reading list on page 21 is to find information (or evidence) that is relevant to your idea (or *thesis*) about the topic. It is important to remember that not all of the information in the sources you have will be relevant. You will therefore have to read *selectively* in order to identify the relevant information.

1.3 Look at the different ways you might want to read a text in the table below. Indicate how important you think each reading method is by placing a tick (✓) in the appropriate column 1–5, where 1 = very important.

How to read a text	1	2	3	4	5
Read carefully in order to understand everything					
Look up the meaning of all the words you don't understand					
Check the contents page of the book or journal before starting to read					
Summarize every chapter or section					
Only read the sections which seem relevant to your needs					
Make a note of other sources mentioned in your reading and their reference details					
Skim the whole text, note the most relevant sections, then read those sections more carefully					
Read the introduction and conclusion first					
Browse the text randomly for information					
Read as quickly as possible					
Only read the paragraph leaders					
Annotate or highlight key ideas and words in the text					
Make notes in the margin of the text					

Before you look at the texts in the reading list, you will see some examples of how evidence is incorporated into academic writing and carry out some practice tasks.

Task 2: Incorporating evidence into academic work

2.1 Look at examples a and b below. Which statement would you take more seriously and why?

a) The number of tourists has increased considerably in the last year.

b) The number of tourists has increased by 10 per cent since last year, according to the most recent government report on the economy (UK Government Statistics, 2007).

2.2 Now look at the following examples of how evidence is used to support a point. Underline the point being supported and circle the evidence given.

a) Any discussion of financial markets must begin with a definition of what they are: "A financial market is the place or mechanism whereby financial assets are exchanged and prices of these assets are set" (Campbell, 2003, p. 47).

b) According to Wang (2001), education is the key aspect underlying the successful economic development in a society.

c) Djabri states that operations research is the application of the methods of science to complex problems (Djabri, 2005).

d) As Sloman (2006) has demonstrated, there are two main methods of measuring unemployment.

e) This antibiotic has an immediate effect on the illness (Braine, 2007).

You can incorporate evidence into academic writing in three ways.

- You can **summarize** the content of a text: a summary is a shorter version of a text, which concentrates on the main information without giving all the details or explanations, so it has a 'general' purpose. You must acknowledge the writer, and you should not include any ideas that are not expressed in the original (see examples b, c, d and e in Ex 2.2). This method of incorporating ideas is the most commonly used.

- You can **paraphrase** the writer's ideas: a paraphrase is a rewritten version of a writer's ideas and usually relates to a 'specific' point that the writer has made. You should use your own words as much as possible. In academic writing, this may not necessarily be a shorter version of the original and, in fact, it may be very difficult to make it shorter without losing the original meaning. Again, it is important to acknowledge the writer and not to include any information or interpretation which is different from the original.

- You can use **direct quotations**: this means you use the exact words of the writer, using inverted commas or italics. You must acknowledge the writer (see example a in Ex 2.2). Quotations are mostly used in essays and journal articles. However, an essay full of direct quotations may detract from your viewpoint and make it difficult for the reader to follow what you want to say. Direct quotations are used less frequently in books, because the authors often want to express their own viewpoint rather than to reiterate the ideas or opinions of others.

In most academic writing, the incorporation of evidence is done by using a mixture of the above techniques, but with limited and carefully selected use. All three – summaries, paraphrases and direct quotations – are used by the writer in academic essays as evidence of detailed knowledge. You should also attempt to use them to demonstrate your understanding of some of the most important features of academic writing.

You might summarize ideas generally or paraphrase more specific points, while acknowledging the sources, and use a direct quotation if this seems to encapsulate exactly the point you wish to make. You might choose to refer directly to your source (see examples b, c and d in Ex 2.2), where the authors are named within the sentence, using appropriate language. Alternatively, you might simply refer indirectly to the source by putting the name and date after your statement (see example e in Ex 2.2).

Students often ask why they should paraphrase when it is much easier simply to quote directly from the original. The answer is that it is an academic convention not to constantly use direct quotations. Another good reason for paraphrasing is that it shows that the writer has clearly understood the point being made in the original text. This is less easy to determine if too many direct quotations are used.

Task 3: Referencing

In this task, you are going to practise identifying different ways of referencing.

3.1 **Read the extract on page 25 from the text *Environmental problems and management* by Andrew Jordan & Tim O'Riordan (1999), and highlight the references.**

Environmental problems and management

The origins of environmental policy

Recognition of the need to both transform and adjust to nature is a fundamental aspect of the human condition. While we may think of 'the environment' as a modern political issue that gained popular appeal in the 1960s, the roots of environmentalist thinking stretch back far into the past (O'Riordan, 1976). The natural environment provides humanity with the material resources for economic growth and consumer satisfaction. But throughout history there have always been social critics and philosophers who have felt that humans also need nature for spiritual nourishment and aesthetic satisfaction. John Muir, the redoubtable founder of the Sierra Club in the USA, felt that without wild places to go to humanity was lost:

> Thousands of tired, nerve-shaken over-civilized people are beginning to find out that going to the mountains is going home; that wilderness is a necessity and that mountain parks and reservations are fountains not only of timber and irrigating rivers, but as fountains of life. Awakening from the stupefying effects of over-industry and the deadly apathy of luxury, they are trying as best they can to mix their own little ongoings with those of Nature, and to get rid of rust and disease ... some are washing off sins and cobwebs of the devil's spinning in all-day storms on mountains. (quoted in Pepper, 1984, p. 33)

Environmental protection is justified in remarkably similar terms today. What is dramatically different is the *extent* of popular concern. The critical question which needs to be asked is *why did modern environmentalism blossom as a broad social movement spanning different continents in the late 1960s and not before?* There is strong evidence that environmental problems like acidification and pesticide pollution materially worsened and became more widespread in the public mind in the 1960s and 1970s. The American sociologist Ronald Inglehart (1977), however, believes that we also have to look to society for an explanation. On the basis of careful and intensive public opinion analysis he argues that modern environmentalism is the visible expression of a set of 'new political' values held by a generation of 'post-materialists' raised in the wealthy welfare states of the West. This liberated class no longer had to toil to supply their material needs and set out to satisfy what the psychologist Maslow (1970) terms its 'higher order' requirements like peace, tranquillity, intellectual and aesthetic satisfaction. This was surely a 'post-materialist' sensibility, but at first it was confined to a vociferous minority that tried to push their values onto the majority who steadfastly regarded themselves more as consumers than as citizens.

Other commentators, however, highlight the tendency for environmental concern to exhibit a cyclical pattern over time, with particularly pronounced peaks in the late 1960s and late 1980s. Closer scrutiny reveals that these short-term 'pulses' coincided with periods of economic growth and social instability, which at first blush seems consistent with Inglehart's thesis. Other sociologists have also observed that materially richer and better educated sections of society tend to give much higher priority to environmental protection than poorer ones, with the highest rates among those working in the 'non-productive' sectors of the economy, such as education, health and social care (Cotgrove and Duff, 1980). Conversely, concern tends to tail off during periods of economic recession (Downs, 1972), and is not normally as pronounced in poorer sections of Western society or in developing countries. The birth of the modern environmental movement in the late 1960s certainly coincided with a period of economic prosperity and societal introspection. Whether this led to or was caused by the accumulating evidence of environmental decay is open to interpretation.

Source: Jordan, A. & O'Riordan, T. (1999). Environmental problems and management. In P. Cloke, P. Crang & M. Goodwin (Eds.), *Introducing human geographies* (pp. 133–140). London: Arnold.

3.2 **Decide whether the references in the text on page 25 are paraphrases/summaries or direct quotations.**

Pay attention to the kind of language used. Complete columns 1 and 2 in the table below. The first one has been done for you as an example.

Name and date	Direct/indirect reference	Idea expressed
O'Riordan, 1976	Indirect	E
John Muir		

3.3 **Study the list of ideas expressed in the box below. Match the ideas with the appropriate references in the table above, and complete column 3.**

The first one has been done for you as an example.

Ideas expressed by environmentalists

A Once people have fulfilled their basic human needs, they want to achieve a better quality of life.

B Interest in the environment tends to relate to the condition of the economic climate.

C Environmentalism is a way of demonstrating political values.

D It is essential for the environment to be preserved, for the sake of our future.

E The awareness of environmental issues is not necessarily a modern concept.

F Only certain privileged sections of society have environmental concerns.

Task 4: Purposeful reading

Any reading you do should have a clear purpose. In the case of Project 1, it should help you find information relevant to the project title: *To what extent can the problems of urbanization be met by a policy of sustainable development?*

As discussed in Unit 1 (page 17), it is useful to define the key terms in any essay title or question. In this case, the key terms you are asked to define are *sustainable development* and *urbanization*. You are now going to try to find definitions of these terms, which you will later incorporate into your project. Thus, your purpose for reading in this case is to find information relevant to a definition of these terms.

> **Study tip**
>
> When you read:
> - always read with a purpose;
> - look for relevant information and seek to identify and define key terms.

4.1 **Look at the sources in Appendix 4 on page 123. Highlight any text relevant to the definitions.**

Either underline the information, using a highlighter pen, or annotate the text by writing a note in the margin.

4.2 **Make a careful note of the source of the information, i.e., writer, title, date and page number.**

Summarizing information from texts

One of the key skills involved in using/referring to sources is *summarizing*; this means being able to state clearly and succinctly the key ideas or thrust of an argument. The summary should be in your own words, with an acknowledgement of the source. If you summarize ideas in the exact words of the original without acknowledging the writer, or fail to name your source, this is considered to be plagiarism – a form of cheating. If you change some of the words of the original, or put it in your own words, and do not acknowledge the source, this is also considered plagiarism. Universities have strong views on plagiarism, which is discussed further in Unit 4 on pages 51–55.

How to summarize

- First, it is important to decide why you are summarizing. Are you going to use this information in an essay? Do you need only the main ideas, or are the details also important? Perhaps only sections of the text are relevant, in which case you need to be even more selective.

- Before you attempt to summarize, it is essential that you understand the material you plan to summarize; if the ideas in the material are not clear to you, then they will not be clear to the reader when you express them in writing.

- It is useful to take notes. The first reason for this is to identify clearly the main points of the text, and the second reason is to use your notes as the basis for writing. In this case, the purpose is to write a summary; often in your project or essay you will use your notes as the basis to express a writer's ideas in your own words (with appropriate referencing, of course).

- Write your summary using your own notes as a stimulus; put the original text away. If you write your summary while looking at the text, it will make it more difficult to summarize in your own words.

- When you have finished your summary, you may want to read the original text again to ensure you have all the information you need.

Task 5: Features of a summary

5.1 **Study the features below and decide which you think characterize a good summary.**

5.2 **Discuss in pairs or small groups. Make a note of your ideas so that you can justify your reasons to the whole class.**

> **a** using the same order of facts and ideas as the original
>
> **b** using all the information from the original
>
> **c** using none of the same vocabulary as the original
>
> **d** using different grammatical structures from the original
>
> **e** emphasizing the points you feel are important in the original
>
> **f** giving your opinion about or commenting on the original text
>
> **Source:** Trzeciak, J. & Mackay, S.E. (1994). *Study skills for academic writing*. Trowbridge: Prentice Hall.

Task 6: Stages in writing a summary or paraphrase

When summarizing or paraphrasing, it is advisable to use the N.O.W. approach:

> ● **NOTE**
>
> ● **ORGANIZE**
>
> ● **WRITE**

Imagine you have been asked to summarize the short extract on page 29 from the text *Environmental problems and management*. Using the N.O.W. approach will involve:

a) making notes on the main points (N);

b) organizing your notes (O);

c) writing a summary based on your notes (W).

The four stages below show one way of carrying out this assignment.

Stage 1: *Decide on the purpose for summarizing the extract.* This is very important, because your purpose will determine which particular points you wish to summarize from the text. In this case, your purpose is to use this text as background in an essay you are writing.

Stage 2: *Underline the key points.* This is the **N**ote stage of the summary process.

6.1 **Look at the extract and underline what you think are the key points.**

> Interest in the environment is not a recent phenomenon; the environment has always affected the growth and development of humankind, as a source of materials as well as a refuge for the human spirit. The recent interest in protecting the environment is a reflection of both the demand of society for a better quality of life, which may include using the environment as a haven, as well as the need to replenish sources. The difference between the present day and the pre-1960s era is the extent to which concern for the environment has become important; there is much greater interest …

Stage 3: *Make a list of the key points*. Write the points that are relevant to the essay title in note form. Use your own words where appropriate, as shown below. This is the **O**rganize stage of the summary process.

6.2 **Compare the list of key points below with the key points you underlined. Are they the same?**

1) interest in env. = not just recent; always int. as source of raw materials + 'refuge for human spirit'

2) reasons for recent int. = int. in 'better quality of life' + need to replenish sources of raw materials

3) cf. current interest with pre-1960s = environmental concerns now given more priority

Stage 4: *Write the summary based on your notes*. This is the **W**rite stage of the summary process.

6.3 **Compare the sample summary with the original text. Do you think the summary achieves its purpose, as stated in Stage 1 on page 28?**

Sample summary

Man has always had an interest in the environment both as a source of raw materials and as a 'refuge for the human spirit'. Nowadays, the two main environmental interests are based on the concept of a 'better quality of life', as well as the need to replenish the sources of raw materials. In comparison with the pre-1960s, much greater interest in the environment is currently being expressed.

Source: Jordan, A. & O'Riordan, T. (1999). Environmental problems and management. In P. Cloke, P. Crang & M. Goodwin (Eds.), *Introducing human geographies* (pp. 135–140). London: Arnold.

Task 7: Practice summary 1

7.1 **Read the text on page 30, *The making of modern Japan*. Your purpose is to answer the following question.**

What is surprising about modern Japan's current position in the industrialized world?

7.2 Follow the N.O.W. stages in order to write your summary answer in two or three sentences.

The making of modern Japan

Modern Japan is a nation of contradictions. Economically powerful and prosperous, its future economic prosperity depends on continued access to reliable sources of external raw materials and stable markets. Militarily constrained because of its U.S.-created constitution, Japan relies on U.S. military strength and the benign intention of others to maintain its security. Pro-Western and modern in its cultural outlook, it reveres old Japanese traditions and customs. The contradictions that exist in Japan – and influence its perceptions of itself and the world – are a product of Japan's historical experiences.

From a global perspective, Japan is a unique nation. With a population half that of the United States and a gross national product 40 per cent the size of the United States, Japan must import large percentages of almost every raw material that modern industrialized societies need. Since Japan's evolution to an industrial power did not begin until the late nineteenth century, and since it had no scientific technical tradition, the strides it took to transform itself into a relatively modern industrial state by the beginning of the twentieth century were truly amazing.

Source: Papp, D. (1994). *Contemporary international relations.* New York: Macmillan.

Notes

Summary

Task 8: Practice summary 2

Imagine you are writing the following assignment.

Discuss the causes of the decline of animal species.

8.1 **Think about the information you could extract from the text below to help with your assignment.**

8.2 **Follow the N.O.W. approach to write your summary in no more than four sentences.**

No safety in numbers

In the early 18th century flocks of migrating passenger pigeons had darkened the skies over eastern North America, taking three days to pass by. Hunters simply pointed a gun upwards, fired, and then got out of the way as the pigeons tumbled to earth. When the birds stopped to roost, trees broke under their combined weight. With an estimated population of somewhere between 3 and 5 billion, the passenger pigeon was the most abundant bird that ever lived. Yet by the late 1890s the species was almost extinct. A few birds found their way to zoos, but they languished in captivity and refused to breed.

It was a result that perplexed the eminent conservationist, Wallace Craig and his contemporaries, and today's conservationists often face a similar problem. It isn't that living in a zoo can ruin an animal's sex drive. When wild species experience a population crash they can go into free fall, even though you would think that by removing the pressure of over-crowding, the survivors would flourish. New conservationists are beginning to realize that under-crowding itself can help drive species to extinction. It's a counter-intuitive idea, but it's not a new one: the consequences of low population density were first studied more than half a century ago by American biologist Warder Allee.

For decades his ideas were largely forgotten, but now an awareness of these 'Allee effects' looks set to transform conservation practices. "They alter our perception about the risks facing populations that have declined markedly, even if they are not numerically tiny," says Georgina Mace from the Institute of Zoology in London.

Source: Barnett, A. (2001). Safety in numbers. *New Scientist*, 169, 38–41.

Task 9: Practice summary 3

Choose *two* sections from the sources you are using to write your project. These should be relevant to your project. Write a summary, using the same method you have been practising in this unit.

Unit Summary

In this unit, you have learnt about the importance of providing evidence in academic writing and discovered different methods of incorporating sources. You have also practised summarizing information.

1 Another student has asked you for advice about selecting texts to read. Write three good reasons for choosing one text rather than another.

a) _____

b) _____

c) _____

2 The same student has asked you for advice about how to read a text. Write the three most useful pieces of advice that you would give.

a) _____

b) _____

c) _____

3 Complete this summary about incorporating evidence into academic work with some of the words from the box.

| summarize   express   evidence   acknowledge   quotations   weight   paraphrase   proof |

It is important that any claim, opinion or generalization made in an essay is supported by _____. You need to show _____ that what you are saying is correct. To incorporate evidence into your writing, you can _____ a specific idea from the writer in your own words or you can _____ the content of a text (write a shorter version which concentrates on the main information). Occasionally, you might want to use direct _____ (the writer's exact words). When you use other people's ideas, you must _____ them. This means referring to them both within the text and in a bibliography at the end of the text.

4 Complete each of these statements about writing summaries with your own ideas.

a) Two things I should do when I write summaries are _____
   and _____.

b) One thing I mustn't do when I write summaries is _____
   _____.

For web resources relevant to this unit, see:

www.englishforacademicstudy.com/student/ewrs/links

These weblinks will provide you with a step-by-step guide to academic writing, as well as detailed information about referencing conventions.

3

Structuring your project and finding information

In this unit you will:
- look at how a project is structured;
- learn to identify evaluative writing;
- practise academic referencing;
- practise selecting information from websites.

Task 1: The structure of projects

In Task 1, you are going to look at a project called *To what extent should insider dealing be regulated, and how can this be done effectively?* (Appendix 1, page 109). This is quite a good project, as it was completed by a student who may have had more experience of writing projects than you do.

First of all, you are going to look at various sections of the project so that you can learn some of the vocabulary related to writing.

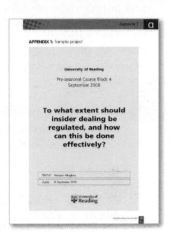

1.1 Look at the parts of an academic text listed in the box below. Which of these do you already know about? Discuss them with a partner and think about where they might appear in the text.

a	the conclusion
b	a quotation
c	a reference in the text
d	a subtitle/subheading
e	the introduction
f	the bibliography
g	the first name initials of an author/researcher
h	the family name of an author/researcher
i	the main title page
j	a figure or table
k	the abstract

1.2 Not all projects will contain each of the elements listed here. For example, some projects may not have tables or figures, if this is not appropriate. Look at the project *To what extent should insider dealing be regulated, and how can this be done effectively?* Which features from the box above can you find there?

How to write an evaluative project

One of the most common problems with projects written by pre-sessional students is that they are too descriptive. It is essential that the description should form only *part* of the project, at most, and that the emphasis should be on the writer's *position*, or point of view. Project writers should use the information and ideas from their sources to support this position.

In order to develop such a position, writers need to think carefully and critically about the *content* of their sources. Once they have developed a point of view based on what they have read, writers should select the most appropriate sources to *support* their perspective.

The writer's position in a text is what may be referred to as her/his thesis. In order to write an evaluative project, the writer should develop a thesis as the starting point and use the sources as the means of supporting this thesis.

Study tip

Description should form only part of your project; the emphasis should be on your *position,* or point of view. You should use the information and ideas from your sources to support this position.

1.3 **Look at the project title below. Think about how this leads to the thesis statement and how the thesis statement influences the project content.**

Project title:

What can we learn from the restructuring of Korea's banking industry?

The title of this project is written in the form of a question. The answer to this question should form the writer's thesis. There are a range of possible answers to the question 'What can we learn …?' For example, we can learn 'a great deal', 'quite a lot', 'very little' or, in fact, we can learn 'nothing at all'. However, based on an analysis of the sources that s/he has read, the student might decide on the thesis below.

Thesis statement:

The restructuring of the Korean banking system should serve as a model for all banking systems throughout south-eastern Asia.

As the student states that the Korean banking system should serve as a 'model', this thesis clearly suggests that 'a great deal' can be learnt from the Korean restructuring exercise.

The thesis might also raise the question '*Why* does the restructuring of Korea's banking system serve as a 'model'?' The answer to this question should make the project more discursive and analytical. In other words, it will no longer suffice for the writer to describe the Korean banking system, because this will not answer the question 'why?'. What is required is an *explanation* of the reasons. This may involve a comparison with other banking systems; it will at least entail an explanation of the features of the Korean banking system that are particularly effective.

1.4 **Study the flow chart on page 35 and think about why a *description* of the Korean banking system will only form part of the project. Then discuss with a partner.**

Topic: The restructuring of the Korean banking system

Title: What can we learn from the restructuring of Korea's banking industry?

Thesis: The restructuring of the Korean banking system should serve as a model for all banking systems throughout south-eastern Asia.

Introduction: Possibly a general summary of all the features of the Korean banking system or a chronological summary of the system's history. The thesis statement usually forms part of the introduction. There may also be an outline of the structure of the project.

Main body: First section: possibly some background information about the Korean banking system that is relevant to the restructuring, e.g., stages at which the restructuring occurred and why it was necessary.

Main body continued: Subsequent sections: an explanation of why each feature of the Korean banking system makes it a 'model', i.e., an analysis of the model. The writer's stance is supported by relevant source references.

Conclusion: Refers back to the thesis statement and draws upon the comments made about all the features described to provide a summative evaluation comment. Possible reference to further analysis that might be carried out on the topic, or a theory about the future of the Korean system/banking in south-eastern Asia in general.

Reading: Critical reading goes on at every stage of the writing process, so that the writer can add to the content.

Text development

Text development

Text development

Text development

As you read more about your topic and take relevant notes, you will be able to make connections between ideas that will help you plan and structure your writing. The more you think about what you are reading, the better you will be able to write an evaluative report.

Task 4: Choosing sources

We are now going to look at why the texts in Appendix 4 were chosen for you to refer to when completing your first project. Those students not completing this project will also benefit from the analysis.

4.1 **Look at the example notes below, analyzing the text *Settlement changes in LEDCs* from Appendix 4 (pages 127–131). Check the five reasons using the text reference and the text itself. Evaluate each reason and discuss with a partner.**

TEXT	Bilham–Boult, A., Blades, H., Hancock, J., Keeling, W. & Ridout, M. (1999). People, places and themes. Oxford: Heinemann.
Why it was chosen	• It was published in the last 10 years. • It was published by an established publishing company: Heinemann. • It contains various case studies dealing with the problems of urbanization and how to solve these problems. • Readers can compare the situation in different cities in different parts of the world. This gives them the opportunity to discuss the contents, not simply describe them. • It contains some useful photographs and tables.

4.2 **Make similar notes of your own on three of the other texts from Appendix 4. Be prepared to compare and discuss your notes.**

TEXT	
Why it was chosen	

TEXT	
Why it was chosen	

TEXT	
Why it was chosen	

Task 5: Finding information

Finding information in textbooks

Many students experience difficulties in choosing the most appropriate texts to read when beginning their academic studies. This is because there seem to be so many texts they have to read to find information and ideas they want. Time becomes a real matter of concern as deadlines for completing assignments draw closer.

You are more likely to find what you are looking for if you have a clear idea of your purpose, as mentioned already. If you have a clear focus, you can look for the specific type of information you need. Textbooks are one source; you may find several textbooks that could interest you, and you can follow a particular procedure to determine the usefulness of each one and save time. This is the first stage in reading critically.

Task 10: Writing a bibliography

10.1 Look at the bibliographical entry in the box below. Match the labels a–j with the elements of the bibliographical entry 1–10.

a) title of article ....

f) editor's surname ....

b) name of publisher ....

g) place of publication ....

c) date of publication ....

h) author's initials ....

d) author's surname ....

i) other editors ....

e) title of book ....

j) shows book is a collection of articles ....

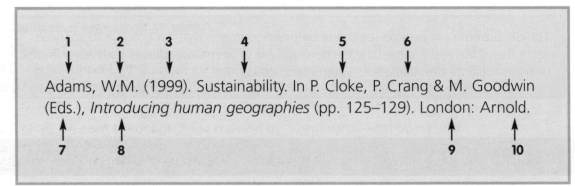

It is the title of the book or journal which goes in italics, not the title of the chapter or article. When referencing a book, you should capitalize only the first word of the title (except where the title contains proper nouns, which are always capitalized).

Now look at the rest of the bibliography, which has been set out appropriately.

Anderson, J.A. (2002). *Going where the big guys don't.* Retrieved February 20, 2007, from http://www.businessweek.com/bwdaily/dnflash/feb2002/nf2002025.htm?chan=search

Cottrell, S. (1999). *The study skills handbook.* Basingstoke: Macmillan.

Leki, I. & Carson, J. (1997). Completely different worlds: EAP and the writing experiences of ESL students in university courses. *TESOL Quarterly, 31*(1), 39–69.

10.2 There are some problems with the bibliography below. Identify the problems and rewrite the bibliography in the appropriate form. Use the sample bibliography above and the guide in Appendix 5 to help you. Check your answers in small groups.

Alan Bilham-Boult et al. 1999. People, Places and Themes. Heinemann, pp. 17-22

Adams, W.M. 1999. Sustainability. In P. Cloke et al. (eds) *Introducing Human Geographies.* Arnold, pp 125-129

'Africa Recovery' E. Harch (2003). [online]. Available from: http://www.africarecovery.org Accessed 18 May 2004

P. Newman, Transport: reducing automobile dependence. In D. Satterwaite (ed.) *The Earthscan Reader in Sustainable Cities.* Earthscan Publications pp 67-92 (1999)

Unit Summary

In this unit, you have seen how projects are structured and learnt to identify evaluative writing. You have looked at academic referencing and practised selecting information from books and websites.

1 **Mark each of these parts of an academic text with U, for _I understand exactly what this means and can recognize it_, or D, for _I don't really understand what this means_.**

a) introduction ___   d) bibliography ___   g) subtitle ___   j) abstract ___

b) reference ___   e) contents page ___   h) figure / table ___

c) quotation ___   f) main title page ___   i) conclusion ___

2 **Tick (✓) the statement in each pair that is true for you.**

a) 1   I know how a project should be structured.

    2   I don't really understand why a project should be structured in a particular way.

b) 1   I can quickly see what is description and what is evaluation when I read a project.

    2   I find it difficult to distinguish between description and evaluation when I read a project.

c) 1   I understand why it is important to write evaluatively when I write a project.

    2   I don't really understand why I should write evaluatively when I write a project.

d) 1   I find it fairly easy to identify the writer's thesis when I read a project.

    2   I don't really understand what a thesis is.

e) 1   I understand why it is essential to have a thesis when writing evaluatively.

    2   I don't see why it is necessary to start an evaluative project with a thesis statement.

f) 1   I know exactly what the purpose of the conclusion to a project is.

    2   I don't really know why it is necessary to write a conclusion to a project.

3 **In each statement below, highlight the option that applies to you when you read.**

a) I find it _easy / quite easy / quite difficult / very difficult_ to read selectively.

b) I find it _easy / quite easy / quite difficult / very difficult_ to keep my purpose in mind.

c) I find it _easy / quite easy / quite difficult / very difficult_ to read critically.

4 **Complete each of these statements so that it is true for you.**

a) The most important thing I have learnt about finding information in books is _____

_____.

b) The most important thing I have learnt about finding information from websites is _____

_____.

> For web resources relevant to this unit, see:
> **www.englishforacademicstudy.com/student/ewrs/links**
>
> These weblinks will provide guidance on referring to primary and secondary sources in your writing, as well as help with finding information online.

Developing your project

In this unit you will:
- find out how to make the best use of the tutorial system;
- learn about plagiarism and how to avoid it;
- learn about the features of abstracts and their purpose.

Introduction

The tutorial system

A tutorial is usually a private meeting between your teacher (who may be called your personal tutor) and you, the tutee. All undergraduate and postgraduate students will be assigned a tutor when they begin their academic courses. However, students who are going on to study for a PhD will be assigned a supervisor.

If you have a tutor, s/he will probably have several tutees. Usually, you will meet with your tutor to discuss academic issues.

The appointment system

Your tutor may set up a system for notifying you of appointments by e-mail or through the use of Blackboard or a similar virtual learning environment. Your tutor may decide when and how often you should attend a tutorial, or s/he may simply leave a blank form where you can fill in your preferred time. See below:

Sample appointment form

Date	Time	Name
August 15th	2.15	Suzy
August 15th	2.35	Ali
August 16th	2.15	Cai

Making the best use of tutorial time

Tutorials may last anything from a few minutes to more than half an hour; usually, you will have a specific time allocated, e.g., 20 minutes. As it is your responsibility to get the most you can from the tutorial in the short time that you have, it is important to come well prepared. You should therefore think about things you wish to talk about before you attend a tutorial, e.g., aspects of your project you need to discuss, or any questions about your feedback or class work that need clarification. You should also bring a notebook so that you can make a brief note of any information or advice you get. However, you will not have time to write down everything during the tutorial – just headings. You should therefore make notes immediately after the tutorial while the information related to your discussion is still fresh in your mind.

Task 1: Preparing for tutorials

Imagine that you have just received the feedback sheet below from your project teacher after completing the first draft of a project.

Study the feedback sheet. Then prepare a set of questions you would like information or advice about during a 20-minute tutorial.

To what extent can the problems of urban development be met by a policy of sustainable development?

Content	You have lots of information here, but your essay is still very descriptive. Think about what you have been reading – what is your opinion about it?
Organization	Try to link the introduction and conclusion to the main body of the text. At the moment they seem like separate paragraphs. For example, in the conclusion you could refer to what you have covered in the main body.
Language	Check the grammatical use of 'according to'. Check how to use the present perfect tense – you still confuse this with the past simple.
Presentation of work	Make sure you have used the correct font size for headings. You have not used the appropriate style in the main body of your text.
Use of sources	You use sources on the first page – but then you don't use any more. Any idea that comes from a source you have used must be referenced. What happened to your list of references at the end?

Avoiding plagiarism

You are now familiar with referencing and why it is important in academic writing. However, sometimes when you are summarizing or paraphrasing ideas, even if the source is acknowledged, the way you write may be too similar to the original to be acceptable.

You therefore need to use your own words as far as possible to avoid this problem. Obviously, there may be certain specialist words or key words in the original text that you need to use in order to explain concepts or ideas. But it is important to avoid writing something that is too close to the original, even if you think the writer can express the ideas much better than you can.

Writing from your notes rather than directly from the reading text will help with this. Try following the steps below.

- Take notes of the information you might use.

- Organize your ideas about the information and, if possible, explain them to someone else. If you cannot clearly explain the text you have read, you may not have fully understood it.

- Based on your notes, write up the information you need for your project.

Remember the N.O.W. approach from Unit 2 (page 28).

Task 3: Avoiding plagiarism

3.1 **Look at the following reasons that students might give for plagiarizing. Think about what advice you could give them.**

Note that your advice must contain constructive help on how to *avoid* plagiarism.

a) I didn't know it was wrong.

b) I don't know how to use references, or how to cite my sources.

c) I don't have enough time to do the necessary reading, or to develop my own ideas.

d) The text is so difficult for me to understand that I just copied the text and hoped it was OK.

e) The text I copied said exactly what I wanted to say, and I couldn't express it better.

f) In my country, we are expected to reproduce the exact words and ideas of the text or the teacher.

3.2 **Discuss your ideas with another student and agree a common strategy. Then write your advice in the box below each reason.**

Advice on avoiding plagiarism

a) Lack of awareness of rules:

b) Lack of familiarity with how to reference:

c) Lack of time:

d) Level of difficulty of reference text:

e) Inability to express ideas better:

f) Different cultural experience:

4.3 Look at abstracts C and D. Do these two abstracts have the same features as abstracts A and B?

Which other features of abstracts do they contain? Refer to the list on page 57.

Abstract C

This project describes the development of China's securities market while analyzng its shortcomings. It also discusses some recently proposed solutions. During the last ten years, significant progress has been made in a very short time in terms of the market scale and trading facilities, even by Western standards. This project describes the main achievements in China's securities market. However, this market has not achieved full credibility due to problems, such as an inefficient regulatory framework, high speculation, corporate governance deficiency and undue government intervention. To deal with these problems, several methods are being considered, which include the government changing the labour laws, the introduction of new initiatives, and the strengthening of self-regulation in the supervision process. The government will also ensure that this legislation is enforced.

Abstract D

Banking has developed over the last 300 years. Due to advances in technology, banks can provide a variety of products for their customers. In 1947, banks began to issue credit cards. In the last 20 years, they have become their most advanced financial product. In Taiwan, major development of credit cards began in 1983. However, only three banks are making a profit in the credit card market. It is very important, therefore, for Taiwanese banking to develop an understanding of the credit card system used in the West. This paper will begin with an introduction to the credit card business, and then describe early developments in the industry in certain Western countries. Secondly, the recent developments in the Taiwanese credit card market are addressed. Finally, the extent to which Taiwanese banks should absorb Western practices in promoting their credit card business is discussed.

4.4 Now read Abstract E. Which features does it *not* contain?

Abstract E

With the steady development of economic globalization, risk has become a controversial issue for financial institutions and non-financial firms. The management goals for banking or individual firms are no longer simply to gain profits but to try to control risk in order to gain maximum profits. This project aims to discuss the important role of managing risk and show the most effective way to manage it. Firstly, a definition of risk is provided, as well as a classification of the forms of risk. The project then goes on to discuss the different financial instruments used to manage risk, followed by an evaluation of the economic effect of risk management for financial institutions. It concludes by suggesting that risk cannot be fully avoided because the world is always changing and so is the financial environment.

4.5 Each of the above abstracts (A–E) refers to a project written by a former pre-sessional student. Based on your reading of each abstract, suggest what you think the titles of the projects were.

The title for Abstract A is given as an example.

Abstract	Possible title
A	*The potential provided by computer-based testing*
B	
C	
D	
E	

Unit Summary

In this unit, you have learnt about the tutorial system and how best to use it. You have also discovered more about plagiarism and how to avoid it. Finally, you have learnt about the features and purpose of abstracts.

1 **Mark each of these statements true (T) or false (F).**

a) You will probably be your tutor's only tutee. ___

b) You can organize a tutorial with your tutor whenever you like. ___

c) Tutorials usually have a fixed duration. ___

d) Your tutor will decide what to talk about during a tutorial, so you don't need to prepare for it. ___

e) Sometimes it's a good idea to make notes during a tutorial. ___

2 **Write three things that you might want to talk about during a tutorial.**

a) _____

b) _____

c) _____

3 **Answer these questions about plagiarism.**

a) Which Latin word does the word *plagiarism* come from? _____

b) If you plagiarize, what exactly are you stealing? _____

c) What do you think is the most common reason why students plagiarize? _____

_____

d) What are the possible consequences of plagiarizing? _____

_____

e) If you paraphrase the ideas that you use as a source, does it always mean that you avoid

plagiarism? _____

f) Suggest some possible ways of avoiding plagiarism.

_____

_____

4   **Complete these statements about abstracts. Imagine you are giving advice to another student.**

a)   An abstract is _____

_____

b)   Abstracts are very useful because _____

_____

c)   Three typical features of abstracts are _____

_____

_____

For web resources relevant to this unit, see:

www.englishforacademicstudy.com/student/ewrs/links

These weblinks will provide you with information on what plagiarism is and how to avoid it, as well as a guide to writing an abstract.

5 Developing a focus

In this unit you will:
- learn how to choose a topic;
- practise narrowing down the topic to establish a focus;
- come up with a working title;
- consolidate some of the skills you have been developing while completing Project 1.

Introduction

One of the most challenging aspects of working on a project is establishing a title and deciding exactly what you will work on. It needs to be a topic that you can narrow down enough to establish a clear focus, so that the project is not too general. This is not always easy to do, as you may be interested in many aspects of a topic. However, by isolating one particular aspect, you can explore a subject in more depth, which is what is required in your academic work.

You will have encountered the first steps to writing a title in Unit 1, Task 6. These included:

- choosing a topic;
- brainstorming ideas;
- narrowing the focus by asking yourself questions;
- establishing a working title which is flexible and developmental;
- choosing some of your sources by looking at journals, books and websites.

We will look at this area in more depth in the tasks that follow.

Task 1: Choosing a topic for your extended essay

Choosing a topic requires careful consideration; as you are working in your own subject area, you need to display a level of specialized knowledge that shows you have a deeper understanding of the subject. At the same time, you need to consider who your reader is.

Study steps a–h for the process of choosing a topic. Put them in the appropriate order by numbering the list 1–8.

a) Decide how practical it is to work on this topic. ▢

b) Find something in your subject area you are interested in. ▢

c) Summarize your project idea in one sentence. ▢

d) Decide how much you already know about the topic. ▢

e) Talk about your ideas. ▢

f) Think about a possible working title. ▢

g) Look for sources. ▢

h) Make a plan. ▢

Study tip

- Think about your reader – make sure your work is accessible to anyone who is interested.

- Your reader should not need to be an expert in the field to understand your ideas, but you should write as an expert.

Task 2: Developing a topic

Look at the following essay titles. Write the letters a–i where you think they should go in the box below, according to how general or specific each title is.

a) *Bangladesh under water: what made it happen?*

b) *How to combat climate change*

c) *Three results of global warming in China*

d) *Increased rainfall: a sign of future weather*

e) *The causes and effects of global warming*

f) *The melting poles: the greatest danger from climate change*

g) *What is global warming?*

h) *The economic effects of climate change*

i) *The effect of temperature increases on maize production*

Most general ➡	⬅ General/Specific ➡	⬅ Most specific

Task 3: Establishing a focus

There are three stages in producing a project: *planning*, *researching* and *writing up*. In each of these stages, there are a number of smaller steps.

One way to establish a focus for your topic is to ask yourself questions about it. For example, *tourism* is a very general topic. In order to narrow it down, you could ask yourself some specific *Wh–* questions: *Why? Who? What? Where? When? Which? How?*

Note that you may not need to ask all these questions about each topic.

Example questions:

- Why is tourism important?

- Who is affected by tourism?

- What is tourism?

- Where does tourism have most impact?

- Which countries are most dependent on tourism?

- How is tourism affecting native culture?

3.1 Make a list of your own questions for the following topic, based on the examples given above.

The education system in Argentina

_____

_____

_____

_____

_____

_____

_____

_____

_____

_____

_____

_____

_____

_____

3.2 Here are some general subjects chosen by students. How could you change them, using questions like those above, to make each topic more specific or focused?

- Problems in the Chinese economy
- The economy of Taiwan
- Cybernetics
- The United Nations
- Genetically modified (GM) food
- Deforestation in Nepal
- Future developments in human health

> **Study tip**
>
> Your essay topic must have focus, so ask yourself specific questions about the topic, such as: *Why? Who? What? Where? When? Which?* and *How?*

Task 4: Establishing a working title

A working title is a title that you initially think of in order to establish a focus for your research and writing. However, as you read and become more involved in the subject of your project, your viewpoint may change. You may decide to change your original plan, and this will affect your final title. This is all part of the process of developing your ideas, and thus part of fine-tuning your research skills.

4.1 **Study the following example of a working title and think about why it has changed from the original.**

The pre-sessional student who created this working title felt that the original one was too general. The student experimented with a second working title before arriving at the third and final title.

> *Pollution and its relationship with people and the environment*

⬇

> *The social and environmental impact of pollution*

⬇

> *The environmental impact of pollution in urban areas*

4.2 **Look at the titles below. Decide why these titles are too general, then rewrite them to make them more specific. This will give the essay more focus.**

a) *Economics has a fundamental impact on our lives*

_____

_____

_____

b) *The origin of genetic engineering*

_____

_____

_____

c) *The effect of technology on society*

_____

_____

_____

4.3 **Now choose two topics related to your subject area and develop your own working titles, going through the stages on page 62.**

You do not need to write projects on these titles, but the task will give you practice in focusing on specific areas. This will help you to be more precise when you write.

_____

_____

_____

_____

_____

_____

_____

_____

Task 5: Planning Project 2

You may already have done some reading, research and thinking about Project 2 in your own subject area. Based on this, complete the following plan as far as possible.

What is your topic?

_____

_____

Why have you chosen this topic?

_____

_____

_____

_____

Key questions (What do you want to find out about this topic?)

_____

_____

_____

_____

_____

_____

What is your focus and/or working title?

_____

_____

_____

_____

_____

Thesis statement

_____

_____

_____

_____

_____

_____

_____

Specific title*

_____

_____

_____

* This may develop later, or you may not know this until you have carried out some research in the library or online.

Unit Summary

In this unit, you have learnt how to choose a topic for a project, how to narrow down the topic to establish a focus and how to create a working title.

1 **Complete each sentence (a–e) with the correct ending (1–6). You will not use one of the endings.**

a) If I choose a topic that is too general, ☐

b) If I choose a topic that is too specialized, ☐

c) If I isolate one aspect of a general topic, ☐

d) If I choose a topic I already know about, ☐

e) If I display too much specialist knowledge, ☐

1 I might find it difficult to gather enough information.

2 it might be difficult to choose which information to use.

3 my project will not be accessible to the average reader.

4 I will understand the information I use better.

5 I can explore it in more depth.

6 it will be difficult to establish a clear focus.

2 **A student has asked you for advice about establishing a focus for his project. Answer his questions below.**

a) Why is it important to establish a focus when choosing a topic for a project?

_____

b) How can I make a very general topic more specific?

_____

3 **Delete the wrong option in each of these statements about establishing a working title.**

a) Having a working title helps the writer to *finish a project / establish a focus*.

b) A working title *very rarely / frequently* changes as a project develops.

c) If a working title changes, it usually goes from *being general to being specific / being specific to being general*.

4 **Complete this statement so that it is true for you.**

In this unit, the most important thing I have learnt about project writing is _____

_____

_____.

For web resources relevant to this unit, see:
www.englishforacademicstudy.com/student/ewrs/links

These weblinks will provide tips on how to narrow down your essay topic and write a thesis statement, as well as a clarification of the role of the thesis statement.

6 Introductions, conclusions and definitions

In this unit you will:
- analyze the features of introductions;
- analyze the features of conclusions;
- analyze the features of definitions;
- identify the language of each of these components in a typical academic text.

Introduction

Writing introductions

While writing an academic text such as a project, it is important to think about the structure and to focus on individual components of the text, such as introductions and conclusions. The introduction is important; as the first part of your essay, it sets the tone for the reader by giving some idea of the content and the writer's position, and suggests how the piece of work is organized.

These are some of the key features that can be included in an introduction:

a) an introduction to the topic of your essay;

b) background information about your topic;

c) justification for your choice of topic focus;

d) an outline of the structure of the essay;

e) definitions of key terms related to the topic;

f) your thesis statement (your viewpoint or perspective);

g) your purpose in writing the essay.

Task 1: Features of introductions

1.1 **Discuss the features of Introduction 1, from the work of a pre-sessional student, with a partner. Then look at how certain features can be identified using Table 1 on page 71.**

Introduction 1

The application of renewable energy technology in remote areas

Our life is heavily dependent on the supply of energy. After World War II, especially, developed countries received the great benefits of electricity. However, today more than 30% of the global population still live in off-grid areas, without electricity. This is mostly in developing countries or remote parts of developed countries, such as mountainous areas or isolated islands. Economically, it would be very challenging to produce electricity for these areas. As developing countries grow economically, the demand for energy will increase rapidly, thus adding to the pollution problems caused by fossil fuels. Renewable energy technology is the solution to these problems. This essay will first demonstrate the need for electricity in remote areas, and then the extent to which renewable energy technology can meet this need in remote areas will be examined by looking at some examples.

Table 1: Features of Introduction 1

Feature	Example from text
Introduction to topic	*Our life is heavily dependent on the supply of energy.*
Background information	*After World War II, especially, developed countries received the great benefits of electricity. However, today more than 30% of the global population still live in off-grid areas, without electricity. This is mostly in developing countries or remote parts of developed countries, such as mountainous areas or isolated islands.*
Justification	To show the problems related to the production of electricity in developing countries, as well as the pollution caused by using fossil fuels.
Outline of structure	*This essay will first demonstrate the demand for electricity in remote areas, and then the extent to which renewable energy technology can meet this need in remote areas will be examined by looking at some examples.*
Definition of key terms	Not included.
Thesis statement	*Renewable energy technology is the solution to these problems.*
Writer's purpose	To show how to overcome the problem (by using renewable energy technology).

From your discussion about the introduction, it will be clear that certain features overlap. For example, background information may be considered in part as justification, and the thesis statement may be linked with the writer's purpose. Furthermore, certain features are not always included. For example, in this introduction there is no definition of *renewable energy*.

1.2 Look at Introductions 2–4, also taken from the work of pre-sessional students, and identify the features listed on page 70. Underline these features and write the letter (a–g) in the margin opposite each one.

1.3 Discuss your analysis of the introductions in small groups. Complete the summary table on page 72 by ticking (✓) the appropriate columns.

Introduction 2

Brand communication in China

Since China began to develop economically and to open up to world trade in the early 1980s, many international companies have entered the Chinese market. In the beginning, these companies entered the market with confidence and kept their customary management system and market strategy approach. However, they soon found this approach was not suitable for the Chinese economic environment, and they had to find a way to adapt to the new situation. Some of the European and American companies cooperated with Japanese companies, because they wanted to utilize the Japanese experience in the Asian market when marketing their products. They were interested in brand communication, which involves using a series of effective marketing strategies. This approach appears to work well in China. The issue of brand communication, including examining why this approach is necessary, and the steps involved in setting up promotion techniques to promote the prestige of a brand, will be discussed in this project.

Downsizing as a necessity for survival

Over the past decade, an uncertain economic climate and the rapid development of technology have led to an increasingly sophisticated business environment. Under these rapid changes, in order to gain competitive advantages, organizations are being increasingly reoriented or converged. Downsizing (Steven et al. 1998) is a response to the external environment, as companies are attempting to reposition themselves so as to gain a competitive advantage in an uncertain marketplace. Emphasis is on 'lean and mean' as an effective way for organisations to achieve the 'lean' purposes of downsizing. Downsizing is necessary for survival in many cases. If human resource managers lack an appropriate downsizing programme, they will be faced with negative feedback from employees. This will lead to the opposite effect to the 'lean' performance and efficient purposes of downsizing. This project will examine how to present a positive vision of downsizing to employees. First, the purpose of downsizing will be addressed. Then, examples of the characteristics of an effective downsizing process will be examined. In the final part, three sets of data that evaluate the process of downsizing will be explored.

Introduction 4

The development of a global company

'Global' means worldwide. But how does a company become global? Are there benefits to becoming a global company? This essay will first explain what a global company is, and then look at the difference between this and a non-global company. Secondly, the essay will explain global strategy and the benefits of these strategies. Finally, a case study of the globalizing development of Philips will be considered.

Summary table

Feature	Introduction 2	Introduction 3	Introduction 4
introduction to topic			
background information			
justification			
outline of structure			
definition of key terms			
thesis statement			
writer's purpose			

Task 2: Analyzing your introduction

2.1 Look at the introduction for your own project. Which of the features in the table below can you identify? Place a tick (✓) in the appropriate row.

Feature	My project	My partner's project
introduction to topic		
background information		
justification		
outline of structure		
definition of key terms		
thesis statement		
writer's purpose		

2.2 Exchange your introduction with a partner. Which features can you identify in her/his work?

2.3 Now compare your findings. Are there any other features you found that are not on the list?

You may need to discuss this with your teacher.

Task 3: The language of introductions

Look again at Introductions 1–4. Underline any expressions or phrases in these introductions that you think might be useful.

Think about how you might use some of these in your own academic writing.

Example: Introduction 1: This essay will first demonstrate ... and then ... will be examined by looking at some examples.

Writing a thesis statement

The thesis statement is one of the key elements in the introduction. Its purposes are:

- to help to focus the content by expressing a point of view;
- to direct the reader.

In addition, it may determine the organization of the text.

You can use the following guidelines to arrive at your thesis statement.

- Turn the title of the text into a question.
- Distil the answer into one or two sentences.
- If the title already is a question, simply write the answer.
- Ask yourself what is your viewpoint.

Key points in a thesis statement

A strong thesis statement is specific and makes a point effectively.

Example: *Obsessive and excessive exercise is a cause of mental and physical problems.*

Notice the following points.

- There is one key idea.
- The *cause* and the *effect* are distilled in a single sentence.
- The reader gets a clear idea of the *content*, the *stance* (or viewpoint) and the probable *organization* of the text from this single sentence.

Task 4: Identifying the thesis statement

The information above suggests that a thesis statement is a condensed form of the writer's purpose.

4.1 **Look at the text below and identify the purpose of each sentence. Two sentences contain simple background information (B), one is an explanation (E) and another is a thesis statement (T). Label each sentence with the appropriate letter. Then discuss your answers with a partner.**

Coffee contains caffeine.

Excessive amounts of caffeine can be damaging to health.

Recent research, however, indicates that a limited amount of coffee can be beneficial.

It stimulates the brain, aids concentration and may help to limit the effects of certain diseases such as Alzheimer's disease and Parkinson's disease.

4.2 **Read the introduction on page 75 from a book chapter called *New cities, new urban geographies* (Hall, 2001) and underline the thesis statement. Then answer the following questions.**

a) How does this thesis statement help to direct the reader and possibly determine the organization of the text that follows?

b) What functions do other sentences in this introduction perform?

> The only consistent thing about cities is that they are always changing. Classifying and understanding the processes of urban change present problems for geographers and others studying the city. Cities, since their inception, have always demonstrated gradual, piecemeal change through processes of accretion, addition or demolition. This type of change can be regarded as largely cosmetic and the underlying processes of urbanisation and the overall structure of the city remain largely unaltered. However, at certain periods fundamentally different processes of urbanisation have emerged: the result has been that the rate of urban change has accelerated and new, distinctly different, urban forms have developed. This occurred, for example, with the urbanisation associated with industrialisation in the UK in the nineteenth century (Hall, 2001).
>
> **Source:** Hall, T. (2001). *Urban Geography*. London: Routledge

4.3 **Write a short, four- or five-sentence introduction to a topic of your choice below (preferably related to your subject area).**

The introduction should contain a thesis statement.

Task 5: Features of conclusions

Writing conclusions

The conclusion at the end of your essay serves a number of functions.

- It is the final part of your text and so needs to pull together all the main ideas.
- It should refer back to what you outlined in your introduction and to your thesis.
- It is an opportunity to show the extent to which you have been able to deal with the issues involved in your thesis.

Why was the restructuring of the Korean banking system successful?

In the spate of bank crises in Asia, Korea's banking system also suffered the hardest time in its history. Seventeen commercial banks were closed and more than 40,000 bank employees were expelled from their companies. It cost 137.1 trillion won (equivalent to 110 billion US dollars) to restore the banking system. The crisis was inevitable because it was an eruption of deep-rooted problems, such as policy mistakes and poor bank management. However, Korea's banks successfully weathered the crisis. As of June 2002, Korea's banks recorded an historically high net profit, and their capital structures are the soundest in the world. Future prospects are good.

There are a number of factors which contributed to this success. Of these success factors, the following seem to be key. First, the Korean government followed many valuable lessons suggested by empirical studies. For example, it set up prompt and massive action plans, including a huge amount of public funds. It introduced a considerable number of standard global regulations and incentive systems in order to be competitive. Secondly, change in the political power of the time played a key role in implementing strict policies for restructuring. As the new government was relatively free from responsibility for the crisis and political interests, they could undertake firm action. Thirdly, nationwide consensus for changes strongly supported government reforms. The Korean people knew that change was needed in order to survive. Eventually, encouraged by nationwide consensus, the new government dared to challenge the tough task of restructuring the banking system.

Summary table

Feature	Conclusion 1	Conclusion 2	Conclusion 3	Conclusion 4
logical conclusion				
brief summary				
comments on ideas				
predictions				
further research				
limitations				
reference to thesis statement				

Task 6: Analyzing your conclusion

6.1 Look at the conclusion of your own project. Which of the features from the table below can you identify? Place a tick (✓) in the appropriate row.

Feature	My project	My partner's project
logical conclusion		
brief summary		
comments on ideas		
predictions		
further research		
limitations		
reference to thesis statement		

6.2 Exchange your conclusion with a partner – which features can you identify in her/his work?

6.3 Now compare your findings. Are there any other features you found which are not on the list?

You may need to discuss this with your teacher.

Task 7: The language of conclusions

Look again at Conclusions 1–4 on pages 76–78. Underline any expressions or phrases you think might be useful in your own academic writing.

Example: Conclusion 1: Whereas the aim of this essay was to evaluate ... it has become a summary of some researchers' theories.

Task 8: Features of definitions

Writing extended definitions

When writing about a topic, it is essential to clarify your terms, i.e., explain clearly what you mean by any key words in the essay. If you were writing about *human resource management*, for example, you would need to explain what you meant by human resources, so that both the writer and the reader have exactly the same interpretation of the term. You will often find that definitions form at least part of introductory texts to your subject area.

> **Study tip**
>
> When defining terms, make sure you are clear about who your audience is. You need to define any specialist terms that you do not believe will be shared knowledge.

The extent to which you need to define your terms will depend on your reader and your purpose for writing. For example, if you are new to the subject area, then for yourself (as well as, perhaps, for your tutor), you need to clarify some of the most basic terms. As you gain a deeper knowledge and understanding of the subject, and are writing for experts, the meaning of certain key terms can be assumed as part of 'shared knowledge'.

8.1 Look at the definition of the subject *Academic Studies* below and think about how useful it is for your purposes as a student.

Term	Definition
Academic Studies	*Academic Studies is a course that is designed to help students develop some of the research skills required in their future field of study.*

As you will notice, this definition does not give you very much information about the course; an extended definition would be more useful to you. You might add to the short definition above by explaining what students are expected to do on an Academic Studies course.

Term	Extended definition
Academic Studies	*Students work to produce an extended piece of writing on a topic in their subject area, and will also give an oral presentation on this topic. They are expected to read widely and select appropriate sources to support the ideas related to their topic. They work on summarizing and synthesizing information accurately, as well as evaluating what they read. They learn about the conventions of referencing and how to write a bibliography. They are expected to draw on the skills being developed in other components of the course, e.g., practising reading strategies by reading selectively, and working on the micro-skills of writing introductions and conclusions. The oral component of the course is also important, as students are expected to be able to discuss their ideas with both tutor and fellow students, as well as give a formal presentation. Students are, to a large extent, expected to work autonomously.*

8.2 Look at Definitions 1–4 on page 81, taken from the work of pre-sessional students. Identify the features of the definitions from a–d below:

a) a formal definition, e.g., from a dictionary or an expert in the field;

b) an expansion of the definition with an explanation and/or examples;

c) a comment on the definition by the writer;

d) references.

Then complete the table below by ticking (✓) the appropriate cells.

Feature	Definition 1	Definition 2	Definition 3	Definition 4
formal definition				
expansion				
comment				
references				

8.3 Underline or annotate the relevant parts of the definitions and discuss them with a partner.

Definition 1: Language aptitude

Some people have a natural language ability, which makes them adept at learning foreign languages, whereas others are rather poor at it and struggle to acquire a basic communicative ability in the language. A factor which makes a difference to the individual is often referred to as language aptitude. Though difficult to define in concrete terms, it is understood to be not necessarily the ability to learn the language in the classroom, but rather to be able to apply this knowledge in a real-life situation (Cook, 1991). While some people argue that this ability is not fixed, Carroll (1981) believes that aptitude is an innate or stable factor, which cannot be changed through training and is constant throughout one's life. He also insists that it is not related to past learning experience. This implies that language aptitude is not something that is accumulated as we age, but something we are born with. This may sound demotivating for those who are not equipped with language aptitude. However, as Ellis (1994) suggests, aptitude is only a facilitator which encourages learning, especially in accelerating the rate of learning, but not determining learning.

Definition 2: Globalization

The term 'globalization' holds considerable interest. It refers to 'the idea that the world is developing a single economy and culture as a result of improved technology and communications and the influence of very large multinational companies' (Macmillan English Dictionary for Advanced Learners, 2000, p. 603). The term can also refer to the movement of people (labour) and knowledge (technology) across international borders. Globalization can help countries get rid of the barriers to the inflow of technology, capital, human resources and products. Generally, globalization makes the above more available, especially the accessibility of products. It can also speed up the development of foreign trade.

Definition 3: A global company

A global company can be defined as a corporation consisting of a group of people who run a business in different countries as one body (Uniglobe, 2002). A global company is different from a non-global company. There are three main differences between a global company and a non-global company. First of all, a global company should introduce its same-brand products worldwide at the same time. Secondly, a global company must inform its subsidiaries around the world of major management decisions. Thirdly, each subsidiary of the global company based in a different country must compete at a national level by taking local preferences into consideration.

Definition 4: Global

The term 'global' (or 'transnational') implies the centralization of management decision-making to overseas subsidiaries and highly efficient coordination of activities across national boundaries in pursuit of global competitiveness (Yip, 1992; Bartlett and Ghoshol, 1989). Geographically, global firms are similar to multinationals. Both are businesses operating in more than one country; however, they are totally different in nature. A multinational business refers to a company with branches in several countries with little coordination of activities, and decentralization of management decision-making (Bartlett and Ghoshol, 1989).

8.4 **Which definition is the most useful for the reader? Discuss in small groups. Make sure you are able to explain your choice.**

Key research and writing skills: When you give a definition, it is essential not to write a *circular definition*, e.g., 'an extended writing class is a class where students learn to write extended essays'. This is not helpful for the reader who wants to understand the meaning of an extended essay class.

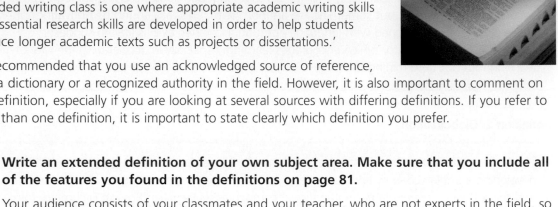

A more useful, non-circular definition might read, for example, 'an extended writing class is one where appropriate academic writing skills and essential research skills are developed in order to help students produce longer academic texts such as projects or dissertations.'

It is recommended that you use an acknowledged source of reference, e.g., a dictionary or a recognized authority in the field. However, it is also important to comment on the definition, especially if you are looking at several sources with differing definitions. If you refer to more than one definition, it is important to state clearly which definition you prefer.

8.5 **Write an extended definition of your own subject area. Make sure that you include all of the features you found in the definitions on page 81.**

Your audience consists of your classmates and your teacher, who are not experts in the field, so remember to use terminology that you can easily explain.

Unit Summary

In this unit, you have analyzed typical features of introductions, conclusions and definitions.

1 **Mark a–k with either I, for features of introductions, or C, for features of conclusions.**

a) background information about the topic ___ ☐

b) a brief summary of the main ideas in the essay, and comments on these ___ ☐

c) justification for the choice of topic focus ___ ☐

d) predictions for future developments ___ ☐

e) mention of further research that might be required ___ ☐

f) an outline of the structure of the essay ___ ☐

g) a definition of key terms related to the topic ___ ☐

h) limitations of the work covered by the essay ___ ☐

i) the thesis statement (the writer's viewpoint or perspective) ___ ☐

j) the writer's purpose in producing the essay ___ ☐

k) a reference back to the thesis statement ___ ☐

2 **Mark each of the features above as follows.**

✓ I used this in my project and think I used it well.

? I used this in my project but I don't think I used it very well.

✗ I didn't use this in my project.

3 **Complete the summary about definitions below with words from the box.**

> examples terms dictionary interpretation
> shared knowledge comment knowledge

When writing about a topic, you must clarify your _____ (explain clearly what you mean by any key words you use) so that the writer and the reader have the same _____. If you are new to the subject, you will need to define the most basic terms so that you understand them properly. As you gain _____ of the subject, and if you are writing for experts, the meaning of certain key terms can be assumed as part of _____. You can use formal definitions from a _____ or an expert in the field, expand a definition with explanations or _____, or make a _____ about the definition.

> For web resources relevant to this unit, see:
> **www.englishforacademicstudy.com/student/ewrs/links**
>
> These weblinks will provide you with an explanation of the features of introductions and conclusions in academic writing, as well as a summary of how to use formal, informal and expanded definitions.

7 Incorporating data and illustrations

In this unit you will:
- learn how data is incorporated into academic texts;
- learn how to analyze data;
- practise using the language of data commentary.

Introduction

Another aspect of academic writing is data commentary. Data is statistical information that may be presented graphically in the form of tables or figures. Data is used to support the information and ideas of the academic researcher. An illustration might be, for example, a photograph or diagram. In academic writing, illustrations should only be used to clarify ideas or information; in other words, they should enhance an explanation. You should always give the source for your data.

Study tip

- Only include data or illustrations if they have a purpose.
- Always refer to data in the text.
- Always state the source of the data.

Task 1: The purpose of data

1.1 **Answer these questions, using your own knowledge and the information above.**

a) What is data?

_____

_____

b) Why is data sometimes included in academic texts?

_____

_____

c) Read the information on pages 85–86, which comes from a book called *Leisure & tourism: advanced GNVQ* (Youell, 1995).

1 What is the purpose of Figure 1.21?

2 What is the purpose of Figure 1.22?

3 What main conclusion can you draw from the data in Figure 1.22?

4 What is the purpose of Table 1.5?

5 What main conclusions can you draw from the data in Table 1.5?

1.2 **Both of the figures and the table have captions that briefly describe their content. What do you notice about these captions? Complete the following sentences.**

a) The language style _____

_____

b) The position of the caption _____

_____

The Development of Jet Aircraft

Fig. 1.21 A Boeing 767

The technological advances in aircraft design which resulted from developments during the Second World War led to air travel becoming a reality for the masses of the population from the 1950s onwards. The Boeing 707 jet was introduced in 1958 and led to a surge in scheduled and charter flights, the latter being combined with accommodation, transfers and courier services to form the 'package holiday' that is so familiar to us in the early twenty-first century (see Figure 1.21).

The Introduction of the Package Tour

The 1960s saw the beginning of the rapid increase in the number of package holidays sold. Destinations such as the coastal areas of Southern Spain, the Balearic Islands and Greece were favourite locations for British and other European travellers. The convenience of an all-inclusive arrangement, coupled with the increased speed which the new aircraft brought, caught the imagination of the British travelling public. The age of mass tourism had truly arrived.

Travel and Tourism Today

Tourism is now commonly referred to as 'the world's biggest industry'. According to the World Travel and Tourism Council (WTTC), in 1990 the industry:

- Generated an annual turnover equivalent to 5.9 per cent of the world GNP
- Employed 118 million people worldwide
- Accounted for over 6.7 per cent of the world's capital investment
- Contributed over 5.6 per cent to total tax payments worldwide

Figure 1.22 below shows the growth in travel and tourism gross output (sales generated) between 1987 and 1993.

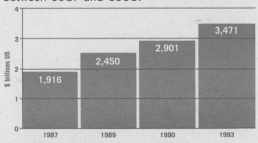

Year	$ billions US
1987	1,916
1989	2,450
1990	2,901
1993	3,471

Fig. 1.22 Travel and tourism output (source: WTTC)
Source: Youell, R. (1995). *Leisure & tourism: advanced GNVQ.* Longman: Harlow.

The growth in total world tourist arrivals 1970–93 is illustrated in Table 1.5.

Table 1.5 World international tourist arrivals 1970–93
Source: Youell, R. (1995). *Leisure & tourism: advanced GNVQ.* Longman: Harlow.

Year	Arrivals (million)	Rate of growth (%)
1970	165.8	15.5
1971	178.8	7.9
1972	189.1	5.7
1973	199.9	5.1
1974	205.6	3.4
1975	222.3	8.1
1976	228.8	3.0
1977	249.2	8.9
1978	267.1	7.1
1979	283.1	6.0
1980	287.8	1.7
1981	290.1	0.8
1982	289.5	-0.2
1983	292.7	1.1
1984	320.2	9.4
1985	329.6	2.9
1986	340.6	3.3
1987	366.7	7.7
1988	420.0	9.6
1989	431.2	7.3
1990	458.4	6.3
1991	456.7	-0.4
1992	481.6	5.4
1993	500.1	3.9

Apart from the early 1980s and 1990s, when the world was experiencing recession, Table 1.5 indicates a steady growth pattern over two decades, culminating in more than 500 million tourist arrivals worldwide in 1993.

The Trend in Overseas Visitors to Britain

Figure 1.23 shows that, despite the world recession of the early 1980s and the downturn in the economy in the late 1980s, together with the lingering effects of the Gulf War (1991), the numbers of overseas visitors to Britain showed healthy growth between 1981 and 1993 (the latest year for which figures are currently available).

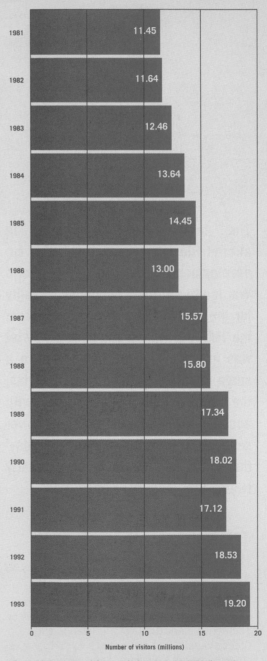

Fig. 1.23 Overseas visits to Britain 1981–93 (BTS figures)
Source: Youell, R. (1995). *Leisure & tourism: advanced GNVQ.* Longman: Harlow.

Task 2: The language used for incorporating data

2.1 Look back at the text on pages 85–86. Find and highlight the language used in the text to refer to the figures and tables.

Example: *see Figure 1.21* (page 85).

2.2 Look at the examples of data on pages 88–89 (Data 1–4). Identify whether each piece of data is a figure or a table and label it appropriately, e.g., Figure 1/Figure 2 or Table 1/Table 2.

The data includes two graphs, a bar chart and a table.

2.3 The two captions below match two of the pieces of data (1–4). Identify which they are.

a) Household take-up of digital television: by type of service

b) Selected media activities that would be missed the most: by age, 2008

2.4 Copy the captions, placing them in the correct position above or below the data (see pages 85–86).

2.5 Now think of captions for the other two pieces of data and write them in the appropriate place.

2.6 Read the text below and add a reference to each sample of data at a suitable place in the text. One example has been added for you (see text in bold below).

> In 2008, the 'digital switchover' began. Data from Ofcom **(Figure 2)** shows that nearly 87 per cent of homes in the UK had a digital television service at the end of the first quarter in 2008, a rise of 71 percentage points since 2000. A digital television set can also transmit digital radio stations. According to Radio Joint Audience Research Limited, the average time spent listening to the radio by people in the UK in the first quarter of 2007 was 19 hours and 24 minutes per week; average listening time increases with age. Between 2001/02 and 2006/07, radio listening fell among most age groups. The proportion of people reading a daily newspaper has also been declining for a number of years. The National Readership Survey shows that, on an average day, less than 44 per cent of people aged 15 and over in Great Britain read a national daily newspaper in the 12 months to June 2008, compared with 72 per cent in the 12 months to June 1978. In 2007, Ofcom asked which media activity respondents would miss the most if they were all taken away. Watching television would be the most missed activity for all age groups except those aged 16 to 19, who would miss the mobile phone the most.
>
> **Adapted from:** Self, A. (Ed.). (2008). *Social trends 38 – 2008 edition* and Hughes, M. (Ed.). (2009). *Social trends 39 – 2009 edition*. Retrieved April 21, 2009, from National Statistics Online: http://www.statistics.gov.uk

Data 1

Great Britain				Percentages
	1978	1988	1998	2008
The Sun	29	25	21	16
Daily Mail	13	10	11	11
Daily Mirror	28	20	14	8
The Daily Telegraph	8	6	5	4
The Times	2	2	4	4
Daily Express	16	10	6	3
Daily Star	.	8	4	3
The Guardian	2	3	3	2
The Independent	.	2	2	1
Financial Times	2	2	1	1
Any national newspaper	72	67	56	44

Source: National Readership Survey. Adapted from Hughes, M. (Ed.). (2009). *Social trends 39 – 2009 edition*. Retrieved April 21, 2009, from National Statistics Online: http://www.statistics.gov.uk

Data 2

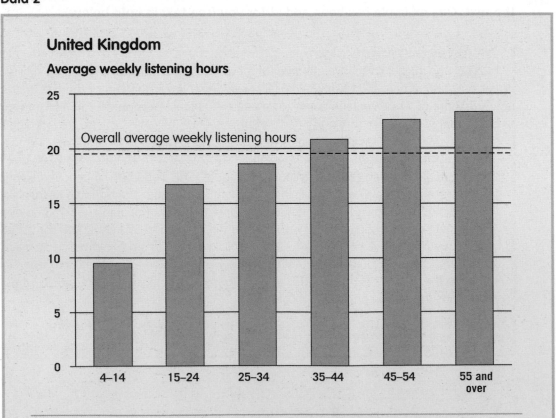

United Kingdom
Average weekly listening hours

Source: Radio Joint Audience Research Limited. Adapted from Self, A. (Ed.). (2008). *Social trends 38 – 2008 edition*. Retrieved April 21, 2009, from National Statistics Online: http://www.statistics.gov.uk

Data 3

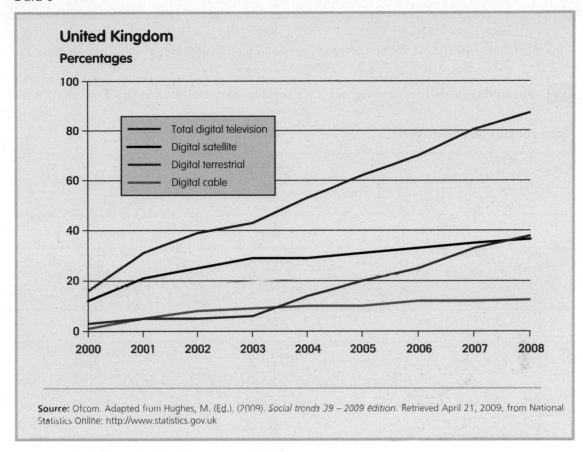

Source: Ofcom. Adapted from Hughes, M. (Ed.). (2009). *Social trends 39 – 2009 edition*. Retrieved April 21, 2009, from National Statistics Online: http://www.statistics.gov.uk

Data 4

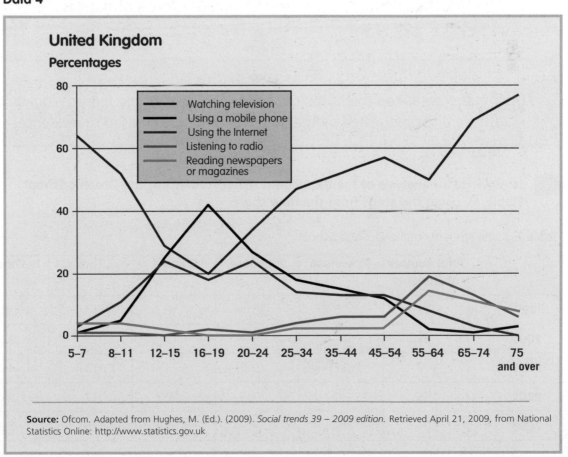

Source: Ofcom. Adapted from Hughes, M. (Ed.). (2009). *Social trends 39 – 2009 edition*. Retrieved April 21, 2009, from National Statistics Online: http://www.statistics.gov.uk

Task 3: Data commentary

You identified several ways of referring to figures and tables within an academic text in Task 2.

3.1 **Study the steps for carrying out data commentary outlined in the flow chart below.**

Data commentary flow chart

> **STEP 1**
> Comment on the *subject* of the data.

> **STEP 2**
> Make a general comment on the *main trend*.

> **STEP 3**
> Comment on some of the *significant features*.

> **STEP 4**
> If appropriate, *compare/contrast* various aspects of the data.

> **STEP 5**
> *Discuss* the data. You might look at the implications or the reasons for some of the trends suggested by the data. This should be based on evidence.

3.2 **Now write an analysis of the data about Asian students at the Oceanic School (Table 1), using the steps from the flow chart.**

Table 1: Asian students at the Oceanic School

	Total number of students	Taiwanese	Japanese	Chinese	Thai	Other
1999	73	15	15	9	14	20
2000	89	12	15	17	15	30
2001	107	17	9	23	13	45
2002	155	20	7	60	17	51
2003	204	19	7	93	15	70

Task 4: The language of data commentary

There are some key words that constantly appear in descriptions of data. These include a core pool of words that can be used as either verbs or nouns. The vocabulary is most often used in relation to data that is presented visually, e.g., bar charts or trend graphs. You need to be careful about the language structure in each case; it depends on whether you use the word as a verb or a noun.

4.1 Look at the table below, and complete Columns A and B as far as possible by identifying the word forms.

Column A: Nouns	Column B: Verb forms	Column C: Accompanying adjective/adverb
rise		• • rose steadily
	increase/increased/ has increased	• rapid increase • increased rapidly
fall		• • fell dramatically
drop		• •
decrease		• •
	stabilize	• • stabilized gradually
fluctuation		• •

There is also a core pool of words used to make descriptions more precise: adverbs and adjectives. These words can express whether a change was, for example, sudden or predictable.

Example: Between 1999 and 2002, there was a dramatic rise in the number of Chinese students studying in the UK.

4.2 Choose the most appropriate adjectives from the box below to complete Column C of the table. Some examples have been done for you. What changes should be made to each adjective to make an adverb, e.g., steady > steadily?

> steady   dramatic   rapid   slow
> significant   gradual   unexpected   noticeable

4.3 List other adjectives and adverbs that you could use to collocate with the nouns and verbs in Columns A and B of the table.

Collocations

_____

_____

_____

_____

_____

Task 5: Practice data commentary

Write a data commentary on the information below, which compares UK employment trends in the service and manufacturing industries.

Use the five steps suggested on page 90, as well as some of the language from Task 4.

United Kingdom

Millions

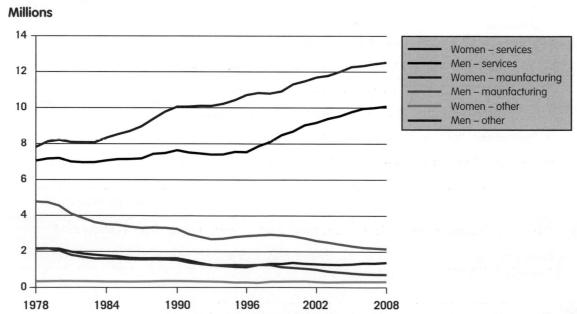

Legend:
- Women – services
- Men – services
- Women – maunfacturing
- Men – maunfacturing
- Women – other
- Men – other

Figure 1: Employee jobs: by industry and sex (June each year)

Source: Short-Term Employment Surveys, Office for National Statistics. Adapted from Hughes, M. (Ed.). (2009). _Social trends 39 – 2009 edition_. Retrieved April 21, 2009, from National Statistics Online: http://www.statistics.gov.uk

Unit Summary

In this unit, you have looked at how data is incorporated into academic texts and learnt how to analyze it. You have also practised using the language of data commentary.

1   **Decide which one of these statements is *not* true.**

a)   Data should be used to support information and provide evidence that information is correct.

b)   Data and illustrations should clarify ideas.

c)   Data and illustrations should enhance an explanation.

d)   Data and illustrations should be used to decorate a text and make it more appealing.

e)   Data and illustrations should only be used if they have a definite purpose.

f)   The writer should always refer to or comment on any data or illustration in the text.

2   **Highlight the option in each statement that is true for you.**

a)   I *sometimes / usually / always* understand data and illustrations that support a text I am reading.

b)   I *often don't / usually / always* know when I should use data to support my essays.

c)   I am *not very / quite / very* confident about using the appropriate language to refer to data in the main text of my essays (expressions like *see Figure 1, this shows, the figures indicate*).

d)   I am *not very / quite / very* confident about labelling and captioning data correctly.

e)   I am *not very / quite / very* confident about using a range of appropriate language to describe data (phrases like *sharp rise, fell dramatically*).

3   **Complete each line as quickly as possible.**

a)   two verbs that mean *go up* _____   _____

b)   two verbs that mean *go down*   _____   _____

c)   another verb that describes trends in data   _____

d)   two nouns from the verbs in a and b   _____   _____

e)   two adjectives that collocate with the nouns in d   _____   _____

f)   two adverbs that collocate with the verbs in a and b   _____   _____

4   **What are the most useful things you have learnt about using data in this unit?**

_____

_____

For web resources relevant to this unit, see:

www.englishforacademicstudy.com/student/ewrs/links.php

These weblinks will provide help with the vocabulary and grammar needed to describe trends, as well as a list of useful phrases for each stage of data commentary.

8 Preparing for conference presentations and editing your work

In this unit you will:
- analyze, evaluate and practise writing abstracts;
- prepare for an oral presentation using note cards and OHTs or PowerPoint;
- learn how to prepare a poster presentation;
- edit the final draft of your project.

Introduction

Writing abstracts

An abstract is a short summary of a whole project. It differs from an introduction, which may outline the structure of a project but does not include detailed findings. You may find it useful to look back at Unit 4, pages 56–59, to remind yourself of the purpose of writing an abstract and the typical features of abstracts.

Study tip

Take careful note of the word limit when writing a conference abstract, and make sure you keep within it.

Abstracts may appear at the beginning of a piece of academic writing, such as an academic journal article, for example. They also appear in conference programmes. The purpose in both cases is to give either the reader or the conference delegate a brief overview of the contents of the article or presentation. The reader or delegate can then make an informed decision about whether that text or presentation is going to be of interest to them.

Written project abstract

In this unit, you will develop your own abstract for the beginning of your own written project. It is best to write the abstract when you have completed the first draft of your project, so this is the appropriate time to begin. The length of an abstract can vary; for a 3,000-word essay, an abstract of 100–150 words would be appropriate.

Remember to include some of the features below:

a) a general statement;

b) essential background information;

c) the aims of the project;

d) an investigation into a particular topic or subject area;

e) the implementation of the investigation in a real-world situation;

f) how the text is organized;

g) details of the research carried out by the writer;

h) what the results of the research suggest;

i) a thesis statement;

j) a definition.

The aspects you include will depend on your subject area and the focus of your piece of work.

Task 1: Features of abstracts

1.1 **Look at these two sample abstracts, from written projects, and identify any features from the list above. Tick (✓) the appropriate rows in the table below.**

Abstract 1

The evolution of foreign management consultancy firms in Italy and China: an evaluation of their localization processes

Management consultancy has been developing for more than one hundred years. It originated in the United States, before spreading to other countries. Localization plays an important role in the expansion of management consultancies. This, according to Crucini (1999, pp. 73–84), is the process of "adapting and translating management tools and ideas to work in a foreign market with a different economic or social background". The history of the spread of management consultancies is first described, followed by an outline of the localization processes of foreign management consultancy firms in Italy and China. Some common problems encountered in the processes are then identified. Finally, advice is given on how to achieve successful localization. (110 words)

Abstract 2

The manufacturing industry in the Mexican economy: a competitiveness model

In Mexico, the meaning and use of the term 'competitiveness' has evolved significantly in recent times. The lack of agreement among Mexican economic agencies about the meaning of the term partially explains the economic situation in recent decades, and has been a core problem in industrial policy. This paper proposes a model to assess competitiveness, and explain its complex meaning. First, it reviews some important economic concepts from the literature. Then, the relevance of the industrial sector in the Mexican economy is explained. Next, the model is applied to a specific situation in the manufacturing industry. The main conclusion is that this simple concept could be the beginning of a more sophisticated tool for implementing industrial policy in Mexico. (119 words)

Feature	Abstract 1	Abstract 2	Feature	Abstract 1	Abstract 2
a			f		
b			g		
c			h		
d			i		
e			j		

1.2 Write an abstract for your written project in the box below. Write inside the box only. Try writing your abstract from memory, without looking at your project.

1.3 Exchange your abstract with a partner. Which features from the list on pages 94–95 can you identify in her/his work?

Abstract for written project

_____

_____

_____

_____

_____

_____

_____

_____

_____

_____

_____

Task 2: Conference abstracts

If you are participating in a conference, you will need to write a short abstract, of 60 words, for example, to appear in the programme. It will summarize the contents of your presentation.

Before you write a conference abstract, you need to decide which aspect of your project you will focus on. The time you have to give a presentation is limited, so you will not be able to include everything. The next two tasks look at some examples of conference abstracts and factors to consider when preparing for your presentation.

Study tip

When writing a conference abstract, think carefully about who your audience might be. Your abstract should focus on the main purpose of the presentation.

2.1 Look at abstracts A–F, on pages 97–98, and match the abstracts to the titles below.

- *Banking systems and management: challenges facing Taiwanese banks*
- *Foreign investment in China*
- *Communication management in Transmission Control Protocol (TCP)*
- *Interpretation and analysis of financial statements for non-accountants*
- *Mixed-use developments in the Kingdom of Saudi Arabia*
- *Situation analysis in marketing*

Abstract A

Analyzing the marketing situation is the first step that companies have to take when they make a marketing plan. This paper will describe the three frameworks of situation analysis and outline how Japanese frameworks compare with Western company frameworks. (39 words)

Abstract B

Financial statements can be used as a tool for decision-making, planning and control by various user groups. The objective of this presentation is to describe how to globally transmit annual reports to non-specialist groups in accounting. Currently, some countries, including Thailand, are facing economic crises. This is owing to businessmen and women not properly understanding the meaning of financial statements, and making poorly informed decisions for their corporations. (68 words)

Abstract C

This presentation explains the basics of computer networks and Transmission Control Protocol (TCP). It discusses the behaviour of TCPs in abnormal events as connections are being opened. Following this, normal closing processes and abnormal situations are explained. Finally, a Finite-State-Machine-Model is used to illustrate the status of the TCP unit during opening or closing of connections. (56 words)

Abstract D

In the history of urban development, the use of the land in one relatively discrete area for a variety of purposes, for example, for residences, trade, employment and entertainment, has often been practised. The evolution of mixed-use developments was based on the idea of compact land use developments in areas with overgrown populations. This practice of mixed-use developments will be discussed with reference to the Kingdom of Saudi Arabia. (68 words)

Abstract E

Since 1997, China has made a great improvement in its economy, and has become the economic centre of Asia. Foreign investment is the most obvious contributor to this performance, and has encouraged China's economic development. The purpose of this project is to analyze the investment environment in China, particularly the development and impact of foreign investment. (56 words)

Abstract F

In an economic system, banks not only facilitate the matching of funds between savers and investors, but are also the main institutions for executing monetary policies. These policies need to be evaluated, and the 'CAMEL' model is one of the most effective ways to assess banking performance. This presentation attempts to evaluate the five criteria on which the 'CAMEL' model is based, and then applies them to the Taiwanese system of banking. (72 words)

2.2 **Practise writing a conference abstract, based on your project, in the box below.**

Keep your abstract as brief as possible (maximum 60 words).

> ### Abstract for conference presentation

2.3 **In small groups and/or with your teacher, edit and discuss each other's abstracts. Pay attention to the typical features of abstracts and discuss content and language.**

Task 3: Preparing an oral presentation

There are various ways of remembering what you want to say, and the order you want to say it in, when giving a presentation. For example, some presenters prepare note cards, on which they write down the main points of their presentation in the order they are going to discuss them. They write the notes clearly, with lots of space between each point, and arrange the note cards in numerical order.

Study tip

Good presenters do not read their notes aloud; they just use them as a way of reminding themselves of what to say.

3.1 Study the following example of a note card prepared by a student who is going to give a presentation on International Relations. In what ways is this useful for the presenter?

CAUSES OF THE COLD WAR

a) Decline in relations – United States/Soviet Union

b) Nuclear arms race

c) Results of World War II

3.2 Discuss what you think about the note card with a partner.

3.3 Look at the following presentation titles, which were chosen by students on a pre-sessional course. Prepare a set of note cards on one of these topics that will give you enough information to speak for two minutes.

- *The retail trade in China: why native enterprises often fail*
- *Modern migration and its economic impact*
- *The causes and effects of climate change in recent years*

Note that a PowerPoint slide or overhead transparency (OHT) can be used as a stimulus for memory in the same way as a note card. However, such visual aids are mainly used as a way of clearly illustrating the key points of the presentation to the listening audience.

Insider trading as an incentive for workers

80 As well as the economic argument for legalising insider trading, Marine put forward another argument, which is that insider dealing should be used as an incentive for the personnel of conglomerates (McVea, 1993, p. 51). He believes that since managers and directors contribute to a great extent to the increase of the organisation's wealth, salaries are not adequate to reward them. He therefore believes that they ought to be able to take advantage of the

85 information that they exclusively possess to trade in the company's shares (ibid.). Otherwise "innovation", which increases profits and is essential to any company's success, would not be encouraged and therefore the company would be worse off (ibid.). This scheme of rewarding managers and directors, although it will increase their income quite substantially, will not necessarily boost the company's performance. An insider can make use of both good and bad

90 news. Use can be made of the good news by buying and of the bad news by selling. Here a manager will benefit from generating bad news to the company by avoiding loss (ibid., p. 52). This means creating a kind of rewarding scheme that is not "commensurate with effort", which should be the basis of any rewarding scheme (ibid.). Furthermore, using trading upon insider dealing as a perk or a scheme of rewarding is extremely unfair. This can be seen when

95 considering that confidential information is provided to an employee as a result of his or her position regardless of his/her contribution to this information. For example, a manager who has been performing very badly is likely to come across price-sensitive information and trade upon it. At the same time another employee who has been performing extremely well may be unable to access the same information. This means that employees will be rewarded according

100 to their position and regardless of their actual performance. Again and for the above reasons, Marine's argument cannot justify legalising insider dealing.

The 'impossibility' of effective regulation of insider trading

Finally, the advocates of unregulated insider dealing argue that insider dealing cannot be regulated properly and it is impossible to have effective regulation, thus it should not be regulated. Insider trading is a very complex crime and detecting it can be impossible in some
105 cases. For example the defendant can claim that they did not know that the information was price sensitive or they may argue that they would have traded even if they had not known about the information (Cole, 2007). This makes successful prosecution extremely difficult. Margaret Cole (2007), the Director of Enforcement at the FSA, conceded that prosecuting an insider is extremely challenging. She stated that not only proving the elements of the crime is
110 difficult but also "the practical challenges of presenting complex insider dealing cases to a jury are immense" (ibid.). However, while Marine sees this obstacle as a justification to legalise insider dealing, Margaret Cole does not. McVea (1993, p. 57) summarised Marine's argument as "anti-insider dealing law is unenforceable; unenforceable law is a bad law; bad law should not be on the statute books". Then McVea (ibid.) criticised Marine's argument by stating that
115 "partial enforcement" on undesirable actions such as insider dealing is better than not having any restrictions. McVea's argument seems to suggest that even if it is impossible to control insider dealing, it is still an immoral activity and regulators should not approve of it by not criminalizing it. Furthermore, despite being a really difficult crime to detect, insider trading can be tackled. This will not be achieved by the capacity to prosecute every insider, rather it may
120 be accomplished through preventing insider trading from occurring. In other words, a proactive approach may well be the remedy to this obstacle.

CASE STUDY 2:
WHY HAS MEXICO CITY GROWN?

It is estimated that Mexico City will have a population of nearly 20 million by the year 2000. Its population density is well over 10,000 people per sq km. Its population has been
5 growing rapidly because of the arrival of large numbers of migrants from the countryside, high birth rates and falling death rates. It is estimated that 40 per cent of its population live in 'informal settlements' or 'shanty towns'.

10   However, Mexico City is not all poor houses. The city has a long history with many magnificent buildings as well as broad highways flanked by multi-storey corporate headquarters. There is an extensive metro system within the built-up area,
15 an international airport and university.

One Internet site describes the city as 'crowded, polluted, and chaotic but also passionate, exotic and beautiful'.

1 Rural to urban migration

20 Factors that push people from the rural areas and factors that pull them to urban areas are listed below. About 1,000 new migrants arrive in Mexico City every day. Of course there are positive things about living in the countryside
25 and negative ones in the urban areas. The 'bright lights' of the urban areas make them more attractive than they really are.

Push factors	Pull Factors
Poverty	Richer people
Low pay	Better pay
Unemployment	More jobs
Few schools	Primary and secondary schools
Few doctors	Health care and hospitals
Poor roads	Cars
Poor electricity and water supply	Electricity and water
	Entertainment

In LEDCs migrants often move first to a local town and then to Mexico City. This is called 'step-wise'
30 migration. However, as birth rates remain high in rural areas and health care is improving, the population total in rural areas is not falling.

There are jobs in the cities – 65 per cent of Mexico's economic activity is in Mexico City. There
35 are oil, chemical and food processing industries. In addition cement, glass, paper, clothing, electronics, household appliances and cars are made in the city. Most of the main banks have their head offices here. The people of the city have very varied ways of life.
40 There are houses for the rich in elegant suburbs such as Pedregal as well as crowded squatter settlements, such as Netzahualcoyotl, which is located on the dry bed of Lake Texcoco.

2 High birth rates

45 When the migrants arrive in Mexico City, they find life hard with little or no employment available. All the family
50 works to get money for food and to pay the rent for their tiny

room in a shanty town. Many children miss school, have a low level of education and many
55 girls are pregnant by their sixteenth birthday. Only 55 out of every 100 children attend primary school despite free education. Few know how to use contraception. Many of the people moving to the urban areas consist of younger age groups.
60 As a result birth rates are high (24 1998).

3 Death rates are falling

In the past, poor water supplies, little sanitation, rubbish and sewage in open drains meant that death rates were high, and buses have made
65 the air so polluted that to breathe is equivalent to smoking 25 cigarettes per day. The city planning authorities with the help of overseas aid, are improving health. They are investing in more doctors and hospitals; there are
70 restrictions on car use; they use lead-free petrol; a metro train has been introduced, and self-help housing schemes have been introduced. These actions improve the quality of life for people and the death rate caused by pollution has dropped
75 significantly (5 per 1000 in 1998).

There are signs that the growth rate of cities in LEDCs has improved mainly because, as women become more educated and they start to use contraceptive methods such as the birth pill, infant
80 mortality has decreased. In addition, in Mexico, other cities have started to grow rapidly.

PROBLEMS

Housing

In Mexico City, as in other LEDCs, housing is
85 seen as the highest priority. Unlike most cities in
MEDCs the houses of the poor are mostly found
on the edges of the city. These are often found in
unplanned, illegal settlements called 'shanty
towns'. Mexico City has become ringed by a
90 series of shanty towns – 'villages' – often built illegally but on public open space or even on
farmer's land. They are built from scrap materials
and are usually one-roomed shacks. They lack
the basic amenities of housing such as running
95 water and sanitation. Some houses have electricity by connecting illegally to the main supply,
which runs outside the town. No one knows how
many people live in the shanty towns.

Water, land and air pollution

100 Water pollution is a problem because rainwater is
not kept separate from industrial and domestic
users. This leads to the pollution of drainage chan-
nels. The high temperatures and heavy rainfall
make this worse. In some cities sewage is still
105 drained directly into rivers. Most shanty towns
have no sewerage system and use pits dug in
open spaces. On hillsides, such as those around
Rio de Janeiro, the sewage may seep down into
other people's drinking water supply. In Mexico
110 City only about 75 per cent of the rubbish is col-
lected by the refuse collection service. In some
areas women collect human excrement to dump in
refuse pits nearby. Illegal dumping of industrial
waste and refuse from the 'informal sector' creates
115 land pollution. Because Mexico City is sited in a
basin surrounded by hills, the air pollution from
four million cars and industry is not blown away.
Car and bus fumes are a problem because of old
inefficient engines and low-quality petrol.

120 ### Subsidence

Parts of 'downtown' Mexico City are built on the
soft deposits of an old lake. Some areas have fallen
by 6m damaging buildings and breaking water
and sewerage pipes. New buildings have to be
125 erected using steel piles and concrete drums.
There have been suggestions that the conditions
in some areas of Britain are nearly as poor as those
found in LEDC cities. In areas such as South
Yorkshire the unemployment level is over 15 per
130 cent since the closure of steel works and coal
mines. Earnings are low and the amount of derelict
land is five times the national average. This is the
area where the film " The Full Monty" was made.

THE WAY FORWARD

135 ### Discourage rural to urban migration

The key thing to do is to improve conditions in
other areas so that people do not wish to migrate
for the apparent advantages of the city. This can
be done by providing employment in other areas
140 as well as by improving their educational and
social services. Better transport allows people to
live out of the city even if they commute in each
day. In Indonesia the authorities tried to ban
migration by issuing people with identity cards
145 and requiring permits to change residence.

Build satellite New Towns to disperse population

Hong Kong and Singapore have built high-density
housing to reduce their problems of housing
150 shortage. They could afford to build high-rise
blocks of flats in new settlements outside the city.
Kuala Lumpur used the same solution but built low-
rise four-storey blocks. In all three cases the new
residents were able to pay rents for their flats.

155 ### Increase employment

Tourism is a key area for the growth of jobs.
Tourists provide foreign currency that is vital to
countries' development. They demand many
services and this creates jobs. Many cities in
160 LEDCs have features that attract tourists. City
growth, increased traffic and neglect can threaten
these attractions, for example the historic colonial
core of Kuala Lumpur, the mangrove areas near
Santos in Brazil, the beaches of Rio de Janeiro
165 and the Taj Mahal in India. City authorities need
to publicize the importance of conserving these
important sites. A key feature of this strategy is to
involve local business people, schools and residents.
The 'informal sector' is being recognized as
170 one way to encourage employment. There are
two main types of informal employment:
- Services such as shoeshine boys, street
  vendors, repairers, newspaper sellers,
  unofficial guides and food and drink sellers.
175 - Small-scale manufacturers of pottery, crafts,
  soaps, traditional ornaments, etc.

Improve transport

The government would like to encourage people to use public transport, but it has to have the finance to fund new buses and rail routes. Some successes have been achieved in Hong Kong, Singapore and Malaysia where wealthier governments had the funding.

Obtain international aid to repair infrastructure

Education, especially for women and children including the street children and homeless adults as well as the mentally ill, would reduce population growth and provide better skills to help with employment.

Introduce legal restrictions and fines to reduce pollution

The informal sector supplies everyday goods at cheap prices as well as meeting the needs of some tourists. The traders are usually operating outside the law and without a license. In parts of India and Kenya the government has appreciated the role this group plays in growing trade and has given some protection to the people. The governments recognize that the informal sector employs large numbers of people though conditions and wages may be poor. Unfortunately the informal sector has a reputation for employing children and illegal immigrants.

The sector is very adaptable and ready to try to supply to most demands. Encouragement of this sector may lead to the growth of more stable industries and the money that changes hands fuels the economy of the city.

Provide self-help housing

These are schemes where the local authority provides a concrete base and water supply to a small plot of land. The owner, often helped by neighbours, builds a house for the family. A second floor may be added as the town gets older. Gradually the self-built estates are upgraded as electricity is added.

Elect stable government

In many cities in LEDCs, bureaucracy, corruption and unrest, including terrorism, have not helped to sustain the quality of life in the area. Foreign investors have to consider these problems when they consider where to locate their production plants. The low wages they would have to pay and the lack of trade union activity attract them but they fear disruptions to production and the safety of key workers.

The Mexico City authorities have joined with the national government and PEMEX (the national petroleum manufacturer) to agree an eight-point strategy costing 8 billion pounds. The eight points are as follows:

- checking car and bus exhaust fumes with restrictions on use until unleaded petrol used
- all new vehicles to be fitted with catalytic converters
- fines for companies found disposing of waste by illegal means
- monitoring of human solid and liquid waste disposal especially on beaches and public open spaces
- new cleaner technologies to be used in factories
- introduction of cleaner fuels
- education about environmental issues
- improved public transport.

Involve citizens

Local authorities have formed Citizens' Councils to involve local people. Similar movements exist in the UK as well. Local people are able to suggest the best ways forward to meet their needs. Local authorities form Environmental Councils to:

- propose methods of preserving the local environment
- receive complaints about threats to open spaces and vegetation
- be a public voice influencing the City Council.

SETTLEMENT CHANGE IN EUROPE

In the EU there is a core of areas with high population density stretching, nearly continuously, from central and south-east England
260 through to southern Italy. This contains most of the largest urban areas in Europe.

Europe was the birthplace of manufacturing industry. The manufacturing areas of Europe developed with the help of their own cheap coal.
265 As late as 1962 only Italy and the Netherlands in Europe used more oil than coal. By 1972 oil had become the main energy source. Founded on the coal-producing areas of the UK, France, Belgium, Luxembourg and Western Germany, a broad
270 zone of industry developed. London's population reached 1 million by 1810 and 2 million in 1850. Paris reached 1 million by 1850 and Berlin, Vienna and Moscow by 1900. By 1994 some 68 metropolitan areas had developed in Europe. The
275 large urban areas of Europe are London, Paris, Randstad (Holland), Rhine-Ruhr and Moscow.

European urban problems

The successful growth of large urban areas also brings problems including:
280 • shortage of good quality housing, overcrowding and the creation of slums
• congested living in inner-city areas
• dangers of urban sprawl using up the countryside
285 • restless migrant populations
• long journey to work
• city transport system under strain
• widespread car ownership and traffic congestion
290 • need to renew central areas
• migration of people out of the tax area of the city they use.

Deurbanization

Since 1965, people have been leaving the urban
295 areas of Europe to live in the semi-rural areas on the urban fringes. As a result the total populations of the large built-up areas have been falling. This has been made possible by improved transport which has made long-distance commuting, by
300 better-paid people, a possibility.

There are many causes of deurbanization, including:
• increased life expectancy and longer retirements
• increased earned wealth of people retiring
305 from urban employment
• decline of traditional heavy industry and textiles
• anti-urban feelings – viewed as crowded, congested, polluted, stressful as opposed to rural peace.

310 ## Reurbanization

In the 1990s a number of governments have become concerned about the decline of their urban areas and plan to make them more attractive.

Source: Bilham-Boult, A., Blades, H., Hancock, J., Keeling, W. & Ridout, M. (1999). *People, places and themes.* Oxford: Heinemann.

The contents of Agenda 21

Section 1
Social and Economic Dimensions: Eight chapters, covering international co-operation, combating poverty, consumption 5 patterns, population, health settlements and integrated environment and development decision-making.

Section 2
Conservation and Management of 10 **Resources for Development:** Fourteen chapters on the environment. These covered the atmosphere, oceans, freshwaters and water resources, land resource management, deforestation, desertification, mountain 15 environments, sustainable agriculture and rural development. They also covered the conservation of biological diversity and biotechnology, toxic, hazardous, solid and radioactive wastes.

20 Section 3
Strengthening the Role of Major Groups: Ten chapters discussing the role of women, young people and indigenous people in sustainable development; the role of non-25 governmental organizations, local authorities, trade unions, business and scientists and farmers.

Section 4
Means of Implementation: Eight chapters, 30 exploring how to pay for sustainable development, the need to transfer environmentally sound technology and science; the role of education, international capacity-building; international legal 35 instruments and information flow.

(Robinson, 1993)

480 within Western societies in the early 1990s. Behind that pragmatic (perhaps sometimes cynical) politics lay a perception of environmental limits, which 485 had itself driven that rise of environmental concern. As Bill McKibben wrote in his best-selling book *The End of Nature*, 'The greenhouse effect is the 490 first environmental problem we can't escape by moving to the woods' (McKibben, 1990, p.188). Sustainability and sustainable development were 495 the words people in the 1990s came to use to express that thought, and on which they tried to build arguments for reform.

Figure 13.3 Smoke plume from UK power station: concern about acid rain was one of the environmental problems that led to the Stockholm Conference.

Figure 13.4 Terraced farmland in Machakos.

Figure 13.5 Stall-fed cows, Machakos.

Source: Adams, W.M. (1999). Sustainability. In P. Cloke., P. Crang & M. Goodwin (Eds.), *Introducing human geographies* (pp. 125–130). London: Arnold.

APPENDIX 4: Source 5

SUSTAINABLE
URBAN LIVELIHOODS

- Jobless growth in cities of the developing world

- The nature of the Brown Agenda

- Ecological footprints and the regional impacts of cities

- The capacity and effectiveness of city authorities as core conditions for sustainable urban development

- Enabling social organization at the local level

Introduction

The proportion of people living in urban areas of the globe is increasing, and particularly in the developing world. Whilst in 1800, only 3 per cent of the total world population lived in towns and cities, it is estimated that by the year 2000, this figure will have risen to over 50 per cent (United Nations, 1989). Although a greater
5 proportion of the population of the developed world currently live in cities, as seen in Figure 5.1 (approximately 73 per cent or 900 million people), the total size of the urban population is larger in the developing world, at around 1,400 million people, as seen in Figure 5.2 (Devas and Rakodi, 1993). In addition 93 per cent of the predicted urban growth to the year 2020 will occur in the developing world.

10 In 1987, the World Commission on Environment and Development suggested that the urban challenge lay 'firmly in the developing countries' (WCED, 198, p.237), due in the main to the unprecedented growth rates, but also to the challenge of meeting the current needs of an expanding urban poor. In that year, for example, the World Bank had estimated that approximately one-quarter of the developing world's absolute
15 poor were living in urban areas (World Bank, 1990a). By the turn of the century, this figure is expected to be nearer 50 per cent, as highlighted in Chapter 2.

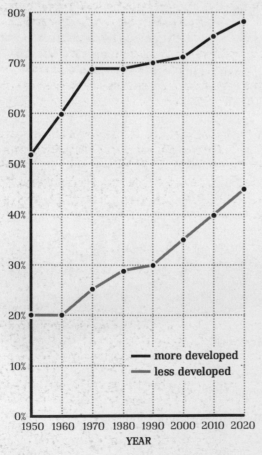

Figure 5.1 *The proportion of the population expected to be living in urban areas.* Source: UN (1989)

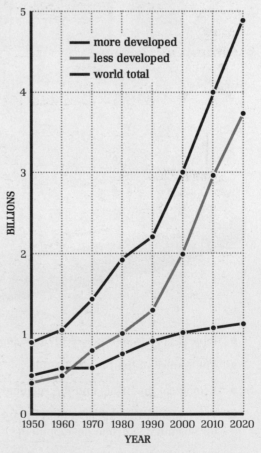

Figure 5.2 *Projected population living in urban areas.* Source: UN (1989)

Cities are central to attempts at meeting the goals of sustainable development in the sense that this is where the majority of the world's population will soon be located, with all the associated physical demands (such as for food and shelter) and the political, social and
20 cultural requirements associated with the adoption of urban values. In addition, city-based production currently accounts for the majority of resource consumption and waste generation world-wide (WRI, 1996). Throughout history, cities have been a driving force in development processes and, as cities grow, productive activities tend to concentrate in urban centres. For example, an estimated 80 per cent of GDP growth in the developing
25 world in the 1990s originates in cities and towns (Bartone *et al.,* 1994). Wealthier cities, and higher income groups within urban areas, consume the highest levels of resources and contribute disproportionately to waste generation (WRI, 1996).

There are substantial challenges for *all* cities in managing the environmental implications of economic growth, in meeting the needs of their residents and for protecting the
30 environmental resources on which they depend into the future. The focus of this chapter is the particular challenges of cities in the developing world, where it will be seen that the unprecedented rates of urban growth and industrialisation in combination with poverty create distinct and immediate environmental problems which to a large extent are not key concerns in wealthier cities. Figure 5.3 depicts a general characterisation of how
35 environmental problems and the severity of their impacts differ within cities at various levels of income. The 'pollution' of urban poverty that arises from inadequate water supplies, sanitation, drainage and solid waste collection is seen to be the most immediate problem of cities in the developing world. These issues have been termed the 'Brown Agenda'. In wealthier cities, the key challenges for action lie in reducing excessive
40 consumption of natural resources and the burden of wastes on the global environment (WRI, 1996). This 'Green Agenda', encompassing the depletion of water and forest resources, for example, has tended to receive greater international attention, because of the relation to issues of global environmental change such as climate warming.

However, such typologies or distinctions should not distort the common, global challenges
45 of sustainable urban development. Whilst the Brown Agenda is the priority for low-income countries, actions are also needed in the cities of the developing world to promote the efficient use of resources and the minimisation of waste, if they are to prosper in future without the ecological impact of past developments as currently evidenced in 'first world' cities. In addition, as emphasised throughout earlier chapters, processes of globalisation
50 are producing a far more integrated and interdependent world economy into the 1990s. Cities across the globe are experiencing change, not solely in terms of their size, but also in respect of the activities they host and the function they play in the world's
55 economic, trading and political systems (Hamnett, 1995). This chapter details the primary characteristics of these processes of change and patterns of urban development in the developing world in order to understand
60 more fully the specific nature of the challenges and opportunities of sustainable development in this sector.

Figure 5.3 *Economic-environmental typology of cities*

Urban environmental problems	Lower-income countries (<$650/cap)	Lower- to middle-income countries ($660 – 2,500/cap)	Upper- to middle-income countries ($2,500 – 6,500/cap)	Upper-income countries (>$6,500/cap)
ACCESS TO BASIC SERVICES				
Water supply and sanitation	Low coverage and poor quality, especially for urban poor	Low access for urban poor	Generally acceptable water supply, reasonable sewerage	Good; concern with trace substances
Drainage	Low coverage: frequent flooding	Inadequate; frequent flooding	Reasonable	Good
Solid waste collection	Low coverage: especially for urban poor	Inadequate	Reasonable	Good
POLLUTION				
Water pollution	Problems from inadequate sanitation and raw domestic sewage	Severe problems from untreated municipal discharges	Severe problems from poorly treated municipal and industrial discharges	High levels of treatment; concern with amenity values and toxic substances
Air pollution	Severe problems in some cities using soft coal; indoor exposure for poor	Severe problems in many cities from soft coal use and/or vehicle emissions	Severe problems in many cities from soft coal use and/or vehicle emissions	Problems in some cities from vehicle emissions; health priority
Solid waste disposal	Open dumping, mixed wastes	Mostly uncontrolled landfills, mixed wastes	Semi-controlled landfills	Controlled landfills, incineration, resource recovery
Hazardous waste management	Non-existent capacity	Severe problems, little capacity	Severe problems, growing capacity	Moving from remediation to prevention
RESOURCE LOSSES				
Land management	Uncontrolled land development and use; pressure from squatter settlements	Ineffective land use controls	Some environmental zoning practised	Environmental zoning commonplace
ENVIRONMENTAL HAZARDS				
Natural and man-made hazards	Recurrent disasters with severe damage and loss of life	Recurrent disasters with damage and loss of life	High risk from industrial disasters	Good emergency response capacity

Source: Bartone et al. (1994)

Urban change in the developing world

Patterns

Whilst the general trend across the developing world, as seen in Figures 5.1 and 5.2, is
65 for increasing levels of urbanisation, there are significant differences between regions
and countries in the patterns of change. For example, it can be seen in Table 5.1 that
the highest growth rates to date have been in Africa which is also where the most rapid
change in the near future is predicted to occur. However, it is in South and South-East
Asia that the largest numbers of people currently reside in urban areas and where the
70 greatest future expansion in terms of additional urban residents will occur. Countries
such as India have very large urban (as well as total) populations, for example. Indian
cities such as Calcutta and Bombay are amongst the largest centres in Asia (as seen in
Figure 5.4) and indeed the world (see Figure 5.5). It should be noted, however, that for
some of the largest cities in the developing world, growth rates during the 1980s were
75 significantly slower than during the 1960s and 1970s (UNCHS, 1996).

In many developing countries, a high proportion of the urban population is concentrated
in one or two major cities. This pattern is more established in the countries of Latin
America than in any other developing region (Hardoy & Satterthwaite, 1989). By 1985, for
example, Mexico City, São Paulo, Buenos Aires, and Rio de Janeiro all had populations in
80 excess of 10 million. In contrast, there were no cities of this size in the whole African
continent by this date (although Cairo came close). In short, Africa's contemporary rapid
urban growth rates are occurring over a relatively small base and are more widely
distributed across many smaller and intermediate urban centres. Indeed, the 'explosive
growth' of mega-cities in the developing world which was predicted in the early 1980s
85 has not generally been realised. Although there is a growing number of urban centres of
unprecedented size, something under 5 per cent of the global population live in mega-
cities (UNCHS, 1996). New kinds of urban systems are also developing world-wide which
include networks of very dynamic, although smaller cities (see Potter et al., 1999). In
short, the actual and predicted patterns of urban change in the developing world have
90 been the subject of much analysis and debate and have proved to be highly varied even
within nations and not always as expected by researchers or planners.

Processes

The key processes of urban change in the developing world are certainly without historical
precedent. In nineteenth-century Europe, people migrated to the towns and cities in search
95 of employment and economic advancement. The industrial activities located in those areas
depended on this process of migration to raise output, and generate wealth. Urbanisation,
industrialisation and 'modernisation' (the adoption of urban values) were processes which
occurred simultaneously in the cities of Europe, and were mutually reinforcing. This has
not been the case in the developing world. Table 5.2 highlights the cases of a number of
100 Latin American countries in the 1960s (a period of relatively rapid industrial development),
where it is seen that employment growth lagged substantially behind that in manufacturing
output. Such 'jobless growth' continued to be a feature of urban change in the developing
world into the 1990s.

Table 5.1 *Urban population change by region, 1970–2000*

	Urban population, 1985 (millions)	Urban population, growth rate, 1970–85 (per cent)	Projected urban population, 2000 (millions)	Projected urban population growth rate, 1985–2000 (per cent)
China	219	1.8	322	2.6
East Asia	46	4.4	68	2.6
South and South-East Asia	377	4.1	694	4.2
West Asia	63	4.6	109	3.7
Latin America	279	3.6	417	2.7
Africa	174	5.0	361	5.0
Pacific	1	4.2	2	4.7
Total	1,159	3.7	1,972	3.6

Source: Devas & Rakodi (1993)

Table 5.2 *Industrialisation and employment in selected Latin American countries, 1963–9*

Country	Manufacturing annual output growth (%)	Manufacturing employment growth (%)
Brazil	6.5	1.1
Colombia	5.9	2.8
Costa Rica	8.9	2.8
Dominican Republic	1.7	-3.3
Ecuador	11.4	6.0
Panama	12.9	7.4

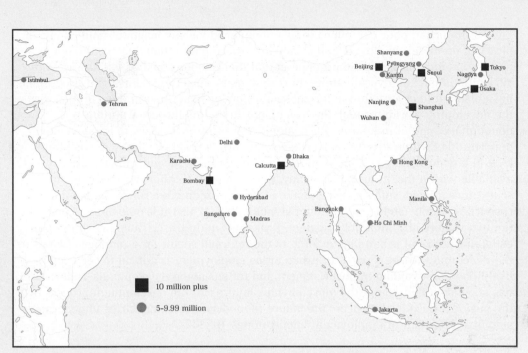

Figure 5.4 *The largest urban centres in Asia*
Source: UNCHS (1996)

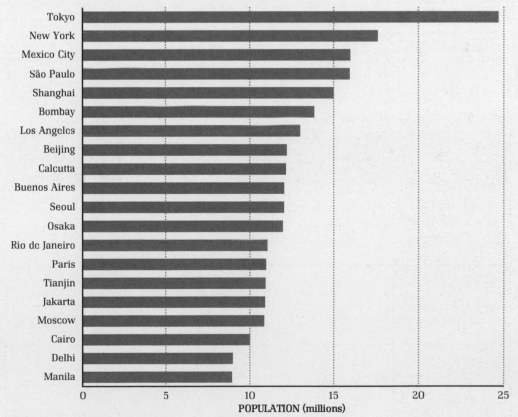

Figure 5.5 *The world's largest urban agglomerations in 1990*
Source: UNCHS (1996)

Few of the urban poor can afford to be unemployed for any length of time. Many, in
105 fact, will be under-employed; either they are working less than they would like or are
doing so at such low rates of production that their labour could be withdrawn with
very little impact on overall output. In recent years, structural adjustment programmes
have also led to contraction in formal sector employment opportunities in the cities of
the developing world, through the loss of jobs in the public sector and the
110 denationalisation of industries, for example. In response to a lack of employment
opportunities within this 'formal' sector, many urban residents in the developing world
look to a wide variety of both legitimate and illegitimate income opportunities
available within the 'informal' economy, the term used to refer commonly to small-
scale, unregulated, semi-legal economic activities which often rely on indigenous
115 resources, family labour and traditional technology. Whilst it is now appreciated that
the two sectors are not wholly distinct (Drakakis-Smith, 1987), Table 5.3 shows the
estimated share of urban labour force in the informal sector for a number of cities in
the developing world. Clearly, in urban areas employment is critical to securing a
livelihood and avoiding impoverishment and for sustained development. Todaro (1997)
120 has suggested that one of the most 'obvious failures' of the development process over
the past few decades has been 'the failure of modern urban industries to generate a
significant number of employment opportunities' (p. 247).

Source: Elliot, J. A. (1999). *An introduction to sustainable development*. London: Routledge.

APPENDIX 4: Source 6

TRANSPORT:

REDUCING AUTOMOBILE DEPENDENCE

SUMMARY: SUCCESSFUL AND WEALTHY CITIES ARE USUALLY ASSOCIATED WITH HIGH LEVELS OF AUTOMOBILE USE AND ARE STRUGGLING TO COPE WITH THE LARGE ECONOMIC, SOCIAL AND ENVIRONMENTAL COSTS THIS BRINGS. THIS PAPER
5 SHOWS HOW SUCH CITIES DO NOT NEED TO DEPEND ON HIGH LEVELS OF PRIVATE AUTOMOBILE USE AND DESCRIBES HOW AUTOMOBILE DEPENDENCE HAS BEEN REDUCED IN MANY OF THE MOST SUCCESSFUL CITIES IN THE NORTH AND KEPT RELATIVELY LOW IN SOME OF THE WEALTHIEST CITIES
10 IN THE SOUTH.

INTRODUCTION

In the post-war era falling energy prices and rising car ownership have transformed cities, allowing the increased physical separation of
15 activities and the progressive spread of urban hinterland at lower densities. The dispersal of employment, retailing and service facilities creates an equivalently dispersed pattern of trips that is anathema to public
20 transport operation. Lower average densities mean a decline in pedestrian accessibility, longer trip lengths and reduced catchment populations for public transport routes. The result is increased car dependence,
25 profligate energy use and global pollution.

The extent to which a city's population has become dependent on the use of private automobiles varies greatly, even for cities where the inhabitants have comparable
30 levels of income. A detailed study of 32 major cities in North America, Europe. Australia and Asia found that the cities could be divided into five categories of automobile dependence. Most US and Australian cities
35 were within categories one and two which have a high or very high automobile dependence and, at most, a minor role for public transport, walking and cycling. Most European cities fell into categories three and
40 four that had moderate or low automobile dependence and an important role for public transport. However, Munich and Paris, both among the most prosperous cities in Europe, along with three of the most prosperous
45 Asian cities (Tokyo, Singapore, Hong Kong) had a very low automobile dependence with public transport, walking and cycling more important than cars.

TRENDS IN AUTOMOBILE
50 DEPENDENCE

The global cities study mentioned earlier is being updated to include data for 1990. The 1980s was the first decade where it would be possible to judge the impact of the
55 global sustainability agenda on cities in terms of their transportation. The early data are summarized in Table 8.2, showing trends.

CAR USE TRENDS

US cities have continued to accelerate in car
60 use per capita (2.3 per cent in the 1980s compared to 2.2 per cent in the 1970s); their 2,400 kilometres of growth per capita in the ten years to 1990 is equal to the total vehicle kilometres travelled (VKT) per capita
65 in Paris or London in the 1980s. European and Asian cities starting from a much lower base grew only 950 kilometres and 420 kilometres per capita, though this 2.2 per cent and 3.3 per cent per annum growth is still a
70 real concern for a sustainable future.

Australian and Canadian cities are showing an interesting trend towards reduced growth in VKT. In the 1960s, Australian cities' VKT grew by 4.5 per cent, by 2.3 per cent in the
75 1970s and by 1.2 per cent in the 1980s. If projected, this leads to zero growth in the 1990s (see Figure 8.3).

Toronto is similar (along with other Canadian cities in preliminary data) with
80 just 1.6 per cent growth in the 1980s (873 kilometres of growth per capita). Figure 8.4 shows the differences between the US and other cities in terms of the growth in vehicle kilometres travelled in cars per
85 person during the 1980s.

The reduced growth in car use in Australian and Canadian cities (especially compared to US cities) may be due to:

- Reurbanization of older suburbs which leads to
90   reduced travel: reurbanization in Australian cities is now more than 30 per cent and up to 50 per cent of all development; it is also very strong in Canadian cities.

- Development of nodal subcentres in outer sub-
95   urbs that also reduce the need for travel and make transit more viable; signs of these emerging subcentres are apparent in Australia but not as much as in Canadian cities.

- Better urban environments which encourage both the reduction in the need for car journeys to 'leapfrog' unsafe urban areas (as in US cities), and more walking and cycling.

- Less dispersion and development of highly car-dependent 'edge cities' which have been characteristic of US urban growth patterns.

Table 8.2 *Trends in the use per person of automobiles and public transport in world cities, by region*

Car use (vehicle kilometres travelled per person)			
Year	1970	1980	1990
US cities	7,334	9,168	11,559
Australian cities	4,628	5,850	6,589
Toronto	n/a	4,807	5,680
European cities	2,750	3,798	4,754
Asian cities	913	1,067	1,487

Public transportation (trips per person)			
Year	1970	1980	1990
US cities	48	57	64
Australian cities	118	93	91
Toronto	154	202	210
European cities	249	290	359
Asian cities	454	430	496

Sources: ESCAP. *State of Urbanization in Asia and the Pacific 1993,* Economic and Social Commission for Asia and the Pacific, ST/ESCAP/1300. United Nations, New York, 1993; Kenworthy, Jeff. Paul Barter, Peter Newman and Chamlong Poboon (1994), 'Resisting automobile dependence in booming economies; a case study of Singapore, Tokyo and Hong Kong within a global sample of cities', paper presented at the Asian Studies Association of Australia Biennial Conference, 1994. Murdoch University, Perth; and Urban Redevelopment Authority (1991), *Living the Next Lap: Towards a Tropical City of Excellence,* Singapore.

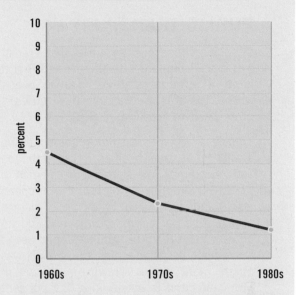

Figure 8.3 *Average increase in car use (vehicle kilometres travelled per capita) in Australian cities*

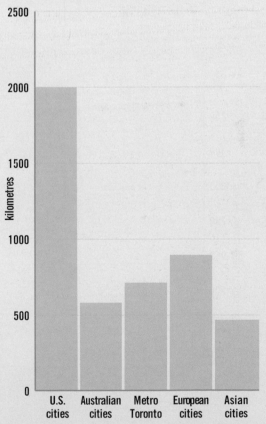

Figure 8.4 *Increases in car use (vehicle kilometres travelled per capita) in global cities, 1980–1990*

PUBLIC TRANSPORT USE

Despite predictions by Lave that transit can never compete with the car and that it is in a terminal state of decline every-where, the actual data from most cities is quite positive (see Figure 8.5).

Transit in US cities is still low but is growing again. In Australian cities it has stabilized and indeed may have started growing again in the 1990s. It grew in Toronto, the European cities and the Asian cities. The average transit trips per capita growth in European cities is more than the total per capita use in US cities. In Asian cities the growth was much more again. Growth in transit in European cities is accelerating (2.1 per cent in the 1980s compared to 1.5 per cent in the 1970s). Such trends are a positive sign of sustainability.

Some of the world's wealthiest and most successful cities have been reducing their citizens' dependence on private automobiles. This can be seen in a comparison between Los Angeles, Zurich and Singapore on how their car use and transit use changed between 1980 and 1990. In Los Angeles, car use continued to grow rapidly, with a decline in the use of public transit, whereas in Zurich and Singapore there was far less growth in car use and a considerable increase in the use of public transit. Thus, the substantial increases in income which have occurred in the past ten years in Zurich and Singapore have gone mostly into public transit use and not into private car use and this reflects their cities' overall plans and priorities to achieve this. Los Angeles, on the other hand, has not attempted to control automobile dependence; here, it is accepted that there is a culture which has little belief in planning other than the facilitation of individual mobility. The use of private automobiles has almost inevitably grown as a result.

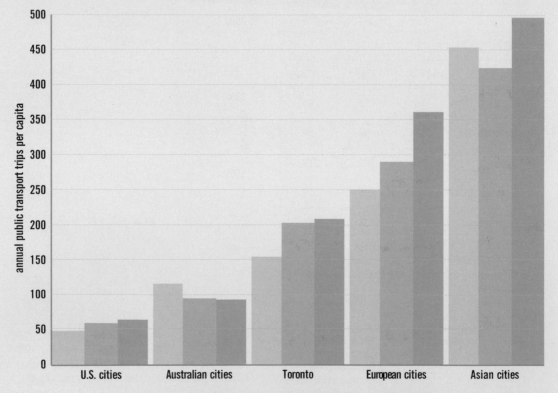

Figure 8.5 *Trends in per capita public transport use in world cities by region, 1970–1990*

THE ASIAN CITIES STUDY

150 We are conducting a more detailed study of the sustainability of seven Asian cities. This is being done partly for the World Bank to highlight further the question of trans-
155 portation priorities and their link to land use and infrastructure as well as the role of personal income in shaping these patterns. Table 8.3 contains the preliminary data. The data indicate the following:

160 There is little obvious relationship between automobile travel patterns and income. Hong Kong, Singapore and Tokyo average 13 per cent of the car use of US cities despite having much higher wealth levels (average
165 of 44 per cent, with Tokyo being 77 per cent of US cities). Their wealth is much more directed into transit, which is on average eight times US levels. Bangkok, Kuala Lumpur, Jakarta and Surabaya have only 10
170 per cent of US incomes and are thus much poorer than Tokyo, Singapore and Hong Kong. On the other hand, transit use is generally underdeveloped compared to the richer Asian cities (about half of Manila is not
175 considered – see below). These are the cities (especially Bangkok) where traffic levels are major economic and environmental issues. Thus, it appears that their wealth is being converted into automobile use on the
180 American model in these cities rather than into transit as found in the Singapore, Tokyo and Hong Kong model. Manila has a very high transit use with its Jeepney system, though its 727 trips per capita is not as impressive
185 when compared on a passenger / kilometre basis, as most trips are very short. As car use grows it is increasingly difficult for transit to remain competitive, thus Manila is preparing to build more segregated electric rail services.

Table 8.3 *Transportation infrastructure and land use in seven Asian cities, 1990.*

	Tokyo	Singapore	Hong Kong	Manila	Bangkok	Kuala Lumpur	Jakarta	Surabaya
City median income (US$ 1990)	38,229	12,860	15,077	3,058	4,132	6,539	1,975	1,975
and % of US	77%	26%	30%	6%	8%	13%	4%	4%
Car use per person (km)	2,103	1,864	493	860	1,562	2,687	383	237
and % of US car use	19%	17%	4%	8%	14%	24%	3%	2%
Public transport use per capita (trips per year)	461	457	570	727	340	337	206	122
% of motorized trips by public transport	62	72	89	73	31	30	47	29
% of all trips by walking and cycling	45	n/a	n/a	30	14	20	43	25
Length of road (metres per person)	19	1.0	0.3	0.6	0.6	1.5	0.5	0.3

Source: Kenworthy, Jeff; Paul Barter; Peter Newman and Chamlong Poboon (1994), 'Resisting automobile dependence in booming economies: a case study of Singapore, Tokyo and Hong Kong within a global sample of cities', paper presented at the Asian Studies Association of Australia Biennial Conference 1994, Murdoch University, Perth; and Urban Redevelopment Authority (1991), *Living the Next Lap: Towards a Tropical City of Excellence*, Singapore

Jakarta and Surabaya have comparatively very little car use but also the lowest level of transit use. Traffic issues are generally leading to higher automobile infrastructure rather than to more transit. These Indonesian cities are faced with a future like Bangkok's if they continue down that path.

- In peak periods, when road space is at a premium, cities such as Tokyo, Hong Kong, Singapore and Manila average 74 per cent of motorized work trips on transit. On the other hand, Bangkok, Kuala Lumpur and Surabaya have a mere 30 per cent, highlighting a growing difference in transportation priorities in these cities. Jakarta is between these two groups with 47 per cent.

- Modal split patterns also vary in interesting ways. Wealthy Tokyo has a very large 45 per cent of all trips on foot and by bicycle, while much poorer Bangkok and Kuala Lumpur have only 14 per cent and 20 per cent respectively. Traffic in Bangkok is now so bad it makes any walking or cycling almost impossible. Private transportation accounts for over 50 per cent of total trips in Bangkok and Kuala Lumpur, while in Tokyo it is only 27 per cent. In Surabaya, the least wealthy of all the cities, 47 per cent of trips are now by private transportation (particularly motorcycles) and walking and cycling has fallen to 35 per cent, down from 53 per cent in 1980.

- All these Asian cities have land-use structures that are built for transit and walking rather than for automobiles. Those cities opting to facilitate automobile use rather than transit are showing all the signs of an inherently dysfunctional system. They also have a much better chance of coping with a world where automobile dependence must be overcome (including the sustainability agenda to reduce fuel use and greenhouse gas production) than US and Australian cities. They just need to invest in the transit/cycling/walking infrastructure. US and Australian cities must also restructure their urban form.

SOLUTIONS TO AUTOMOBILE DEPENDENCE

National and city governments in both the North and the South are questioning the future of cities and urban systems in which private automobiles have the central role in the transport of people. This stems from a greater recognition of the economic, social and environmental costs of 'automobile-dependent' cities that were described above. Solutions to automobile dependence are thus being sought across the globe.

Automobiles and trucks can be 'civilized' through technological advances that greatly reduce fuel use and polluting emissions and increase safety both for the vehicle users and for other road users. Sophisticated traffic management systems can increase efficiency in the use of road spaces and the number of vehicles using road systems without congestion. But, increasingly, even if the incorporation of these advances was accelerated, it is seen as insufficient as the sheer volume of cars, trucks and other motorized road vehicles overwhelms cities. This is especially so in high-density cities that have a low proportion of their total area devoted to roads, as in many cities in Europe and in the South. Seeking to expand road systems to cope with projections of increased automobile use in high-density cities also disrupts the urban fabric and displaces large numbers of people. It was the scale of this disruption in cities in the North that helped to generate a re-evaluation of the priority that was being given to private automobile users. For many of the major cities in the South, the number of automobiles is growing much more rapidly than the number of people, and building the roads and highways to cope with projections for increased automobile use will mean the displacement of tens of thousands (or more) people in each such city. There is also the more recent recognition that people who do not have access to a car are significantly disadvantaged as automobile dependence within a city or region increases since this also leads to a deterioration in public transit and a city in which access to workplaces, schools, shops and services is increasingly difficult without a car.

Despite the doubts as to whether the use of private cars can be controlled, not least because of the power of the economic interests behind the automobile-dependent model, there is a growing awareness of the need to plan to reduce automobile-dependence within cities. Many cities have pedestrianized their central districts; for most, this was easily done as these were historic city centres that originally developed as 'walking cities' before the advent of motorized transport. But there are also many examples of cities which have reduced automobile dependence through innovations in public transit and controls on automobile use in both the North and the South. They include Hong Kong, Singapore and Surabaya in Asia, Curitiba in Latin America, Zurich, Copenhagen and Freiburg in Europe, Toronto and Portland in North America and Perth in Australia, and the means by which they achieved this are outlined below. The fact that this list includes some of the wealthiest cities in both the North and South shows that reducing automobile dependence is possible even in societies with high levels of automobile ownership.

There is also much discussion about the need for public transit-oriented development as the basis for any sustainable city. The link with sustainable development comes from the fact that there is a rapid growth in the number of automobile-dependent cities and in most of these cities, automobile dependence is still increasing. The world's consumption of fossil fuels and total emissions of greenhouse gases would increase dramatically if the whole world's population came to be as automobile dependent as North America, Western

Europe or Australia. The OECD and the World Bank have begun to recognize this and are stressing how transport funding needs to be more critically evaluated. But, in a globally connected world, the reduction of automobile dependence (and its associated energy use, resource use, air pollution and greenhouse gas emissions) should be directed both to cities where automobile dependence is highest and to cities in the South where short-term and long-term measures can reduce their automobile dependence while also enhancing their prosperity and quality of life.

KEY POLICY CONCLUSIONS

Four key conclusions of relevance to public policy can be drawn from the data on cities around the world as to how automobile dependence can be reduced:

• *Public transport infrastructure* – investment in transit infrastructure can help to shape the city as well as ease traffic problems – for instance, encouraging 'walking cities' to develop around light railway or rapid busway stations. There is a considerable range of technological options too, varying in price, capacity and speed and these include options such as express busways that do not require heavy investments. It is also possible to 'upgrade' as demand rises and as cities grow in size and wealth – for instance, as light railways or trams replace express busways. It is also possible to draw on private sector resources – for instance, through city authorities providing the framework within which private bus companies bid for particular routes or areas. But this can only be achieved if public transit is part of a broader policy that discourages low-density developments and unnecessary automobile use. If public transit is left as a supplementary process in streets designed for the automobile, there will be no resolution of the transport dilemma.

370 • *Pedestrian/cycle orientation* – if the goal is to provide for the most efficient, equitable and human form of transport, this means a city with provision for cycling, good walking space on 375 streets and in public squares, and traffic-free shopping streets. Any city that neglects this dimension will find social and economic problems as well as the obvious environmental ones.

380 • *Density* – the need to maintain land-use efficiency is linked closely to transport. Dispersing land uses at low density creates automobile dependence. Dense urban villages linked by public transit creates the opportunity for 385 'walking city' and 'transit city' characteristics to be introduced into the automobile-dependent city (see Figure 8.5, which should be compared to Figure 8.2). Similarly, introducing new and efficient public transit lines into rapidly 390 growing cities can encourage the development of such dense urban settlements and limit low-density sprawl, especially if land-use planning helps to encourage such developments.

• *Planning and control* – all three of the above policies have strong market pressures behind them. But they also require planning to facilitate 395 them. This planning is not heavy-handed bureaucracy but an expression of any city's cultural values, and also of the needs and priorities of pedestrians and cyclists and of children, youth and all other citizens who 400 cannot or do not use cars. All cities have some commitment to this social value. If automobile dependence is not resisted through conscious planning, it will erode or help to destroy most attempts to maintain community life in an urban 405 setting. For all cities, but particularly those in the South, strong neighbourhoods need to be protected from the dispersing and disruptive aspects of the automobile, while in many cities in the wealthiest market economies of the 410 world, the policy of reducing automobile dependence is part of a process to reclaim residential neighbourhoods.

Source: Newman, P. (1999). Transport: reducing automobile dependence. In D. Satterthwaite (Ed.), *The Earthscan reader in sustainable cities* (pp. 67–92). London: Earthscan Publications.

APPENDIX 5: Compiling a bibliography

A book – single author

A book – more than one author

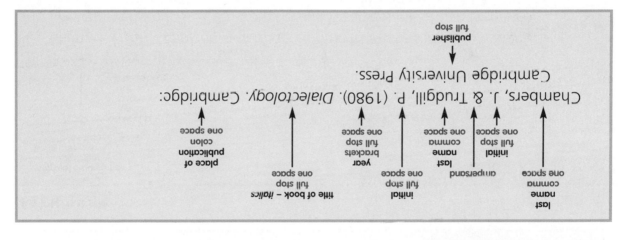

A journal article

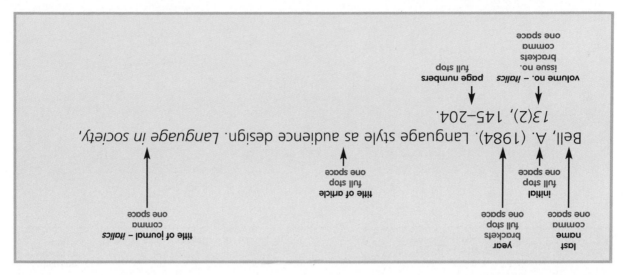

An internet site

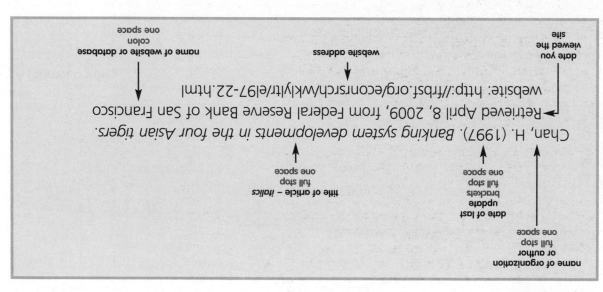

Chan, H. (1997). *Banking system developments in the four Asian tigers.*
Retrieved April 8, 2009, from Federal Reserve Bank of San Francisco
website: http://frbsf.org/econsrch/wklyltr/el97-22.html

name of organization
or author
full stop
one space

date of last
update
brackets
title of article – *italics*
full stop
one space

date you
viewed the
site

website address

name of website or database
colon
one space

A section or chapter of a book

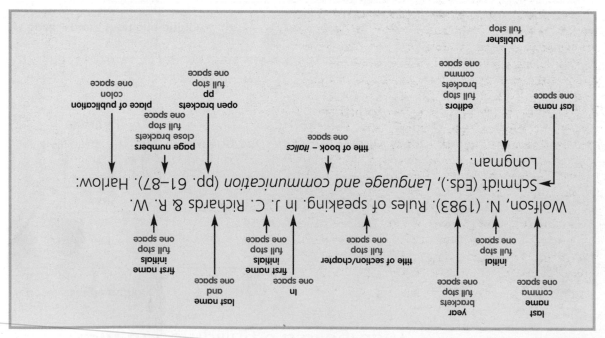

Wolfson, N. (1983). Rules of speaking. In J. C. Richards & R. W.
Schmidt (Eds.), *Language and communication* (pp. 61–87). Harlow:
Longman.

last
name
comma
one space

initial
full stop
one space

year
brackets
full stop
one space

title of section/chapter
full stop
one space

In
one space

first name
initials
full stop
one space

last name
and
one space

first name
initials
full stop
one space

editors
brackets
full stop
comma
one space

last name
one space

title of book – *italics*
one space

page numbers
close brackets
full stop
one space

pp
open brackets
full stop
one space

place of publication
colon
one space

publisher
full stop